TOP

SCANDINAVIAN

2025

TRAVEL GUIDE

Gerald E. Priddy

Copyright © Gerald E. Priddy 2025.

All rights reserved. No part of this publication may be reproduced, distributed, or transmitted in any form or by any means, including photocopying, recording, or other electronic or mechanical methods, without the prior written permission of the publisher, except in the case of brief quotations embodied in critical reviews and certain other noncommercial uses permitted by copyright law

Table Of Contents

Welcome To Scandinavian 5

PLANNING YOUR TRIP 7

    Best Time to Visit Scandinavia 7

    Entry Requirements and Visa Information 9

    Getting to Scandinavia 12

    Budgeting for Your Trip 15

    Packing Guide 17

    Health and Safety Considerations 19

MUST-SEE ATTRACTIONS AND LANDMARKS 23

    Denmark 23

    Sweden 26

    Norway 29

    Finland 32

    Iceland 34

ACCOMMODATION OPTIONS 38

    Luxury Hotels and Resorts 38

    Mid-Range Hotels and Boutique Stays 40

    Hostels and Budget Lodging 42

    Vacation Rentals and Airbnb 44

DINING AND CUISINE 47

    Traditional Scandinavian Dishes 47

    Street Food and Local Markets 49

    Fine Dining and Michelin-Star Restaurants 51

    Coffee Culture and Local Drinks 52

    Vegetarian and Vegan Dining 54

THINGS TO DO AND OUTDOOR ACTIVITIES 56

    Winter Adventures 56

    Summer Outdoor Activities 58

    Wildlife and Nature Excursions 60

ART, CULTURE, AND ENTERTAINMENT 63

    Museums and Art Galleries 63

    Music and Festivals 66

    Literature and Folklore 67

7-DAY ITINERARY 69

    Day 1: Copenhagen, Denmark 69

    Day 2: Stockholm, Sweden 71

    Day 3: Oslo, Norway 74

    Day 4: Bergen and the Fjords 76

    Day 5: Helsinki, Finland 78

    Day 6: Reykjavik, Iceland 81

    Day 7: Iceland's Natural Wonders 83

PRACTICAL INFORMATION AND TIPS 87

    Transportation in Scandinavia 87

    Money and Budgeting 89

    Language and Communication 91

    Safety and Travel Tips 93

    Cultural Etiquette 95

Welcome To Scandinavian

Scandinavia is a place where the extraordinary feels effortless, a region that blends the dramatic beauty of nature with the timeless charm of culture and tradition. From the majestic fjords of Norway to Sweden's serene archipelagos, Denmark's charming cities, Finland's pristine lakes, and Iceland's otherworldly landscapes, this corner of the world beckons with its unique allure. Here, every season brings its own magic, whether it's the Midnight Sun illuminating the summer sky or the Northern Lights painting the winter heavens in shimmering colors.

Stepping into Scandinavia feels like entering a storybook, but this isn't just a land to admire—it's a land to experience. Wander through cobblestone streets lined with colorful houses in Copenhagen's Nyhavn, or lose yourself in the medieval charm of Stockholm's Gamla Stan. Stand in awe at the mighty Gullfoss waterfall in Iceland or hike Norway's iconic Pulpit Rock for views that seem to stretch to eternity. In Finland, discover the tranquility of the wilderness or the joy of a traditional sauna, a quintessential Finnish experience.

But Scandinavia isn't just about breathtaking sights. It's also about the way of life—a celebration of balance, simplicity, and connection. You'll find this spirit in the Danish concept of hygge, the cozy warmth of good company, or in Sweden's fika, a cherished coffee break that's as much about friendship as it is about delicious pastries. In Norway, the awe-inspiring landscapes inspire a deep respect for nature, while Finland's reverence for wellness invites you to slow down and recharge. Iceland's rugged beauty reflects the resilience and creativity of its people, who have turned a land of fire and ice into one of the world's most welcoming destinations.

The people of Scandinavia embody their environment—warm, welcoming, and deeply respectful of both nature and tradition. English is widely spoken, making it easy to communicate, but a heartfelt "takk" (thank you) or "hej" (hello) in the local language will always bring a smile. Sustainability is a way of life here, so don't be surprised to see locals biking to work, sorting their recycling with care, or shopping at organic markets. It's a way of thinking that extends to visitors, encouraging everyone to tread lightly and leave this beautiful region as pristine as they found it.

As you journey through Scandinavia, you'll discover not just a place but a feeling—of wonder, connection, and inspiration. Whether you're sipping mulled wine in a Christmas market, watching puffins on a remote Icelandic cliff, or marveling at the design-forward creations in a Helsinki boutique, each moment will feel like a treasure to carry home.

So pack your sense of adventure, your appreciation for beauty, and your curiosity for the stories this region has to share. Scandinavia a place where every corner is a postcard, every meal a celebration, and every experience a memory waiting to be made. Your journey begins here.

PLANNING YOUR TRIP

Best Time to Visit Scandinavia

Summer in Scandinavia is an ode to the brilliance of life itself. As the snow melts and the landscapes awaken, the Midnight Sun casts its spell, bathing the land in perpetual daylight. Imagine standing on a quiet shoreline in Norway's Lofoten Islands at 2 a.m., with the sun hovering just above the horizon, painting the sky in hues of pink, gold, and lavender. It's more than a sight—it's a sensation, a reminder that life doesn't have to follow conventional rhythms. This is the perfect time for hiking adventures in Sweden's Kungsleden trail, sailing through the fjords of Norway, or cycling across Denmark's countryside. The long days seem to stretch endlessly, making it easy to pack every moment with experiences you'll remember forever.

But summer isn't just about the landscapes; it's also a season of celebration. In June, Midsummer festivities sweep across Scandinavia, with people gathering to dance around maypoles, sing traditional songs, and feast on pickled herring, new potatoes, and aquavit. Sweden, in particular, comes alive with this festival, as towns and villages transform into vibrant hubs of music and joy. Meanwhile, in Denmark, Roskilde Festival, one of Europe's largest music events, attracts visitors from around the world with its incredible lineup of performances and a palpable sense of community.

Summer also offers an unparalleled opportunity to explore Scandinavia's archipelagos. Take the Stockholm Archipelago, for instance—a collection of over 30,000 islands, each with its own charm. Rent a kayak, and paddle between islands dotted with traditional red cottages and lush forests. It's easy to feel as though you've discovered a secret world, far removed from the pace of modern life. And for wildlife enthusiasts, summer is prime time to spot puffins, whales, and seals along the coasts of Norway and Iceland, where the natural world is at its most active and abundant.

Then, there's winter—a season that transforms Scandinavia into a wonderland of snow, ice, and ethereal light. If summer feels like a celebration of the world's vitality, winter feels like a meditation on its beauty. This is the time to witness the Northern Lights, a phenomenon so breathtaking it defies description. Imagine standing beneath a star-filled sky in Finnish Lapland as ribbons of green, pink, and violet dance overhead. It's a moment that connects you to something larger than yourself, a spectacle that reminds you of the magic that exists in the natural world.

Winter invites you to slow down and embrace the cozy, intimate side of Scandinavia. Hygge—a Danish concept that captures the feeling of warmth, comfort, and contentment—is best experienced during these chilly months. Picture yourself in a candlelit café in Copenhagen, savoring a steaming cup of mulled wine while snow falls softly outside. It's not just about staying warm; it's about finding joy in the simplicity of the moment.

For those seeking adventure, winter delivers in spades. Dog sledding through snow-covered forests in Sweden, ice fishing in Finland, and skiing in Norway's pristine slopes are just a few ways to connect with the season. The Icehotel in Jukkasjärvi, Sweden, offers a once-in-a-lifetime chance to sleep in a room carved entirely from ice and snow, while Norway's Tromsø serves as a gateway to Arctic expeditions and reindeer safaris.

Winter is also when many of Scandinavia's most magical festivals take place. In late November and December, Christmas markets light up towns and cities across the region. Wander through the stalls at Tivoli Gardens in Copenhagen or Skansen in

Stockholm, where you can shop for handmade crafts, sample traditional treats like glögg and gingerbread, and feel the festive spirit come alive. Another highlight is the Sami Week in Tromsø, which celebrates the culture and traditions of the indigenous Sami people with events like reindeer racing, joik singing, and handicraft exhibitions.

Even as the cold deepens, Scandinavia's cities remain vibrant and welcoming. Oslo's Winter Festival offers ice skating, cultural performances, and culinary delights, while Helsinki's Lux Festival illuminates the city with stunning light installations. And let's not forget the quirky celebration of the Polar Bear Swim in Denmark, where locals and visitors alike take a bracing plunge into icy waters—a testament to the Scandinavian love for embracing the elements.

When comparing summer and winter, the best time to visit Scandinavia ultimately depends on what you want to take away from your journey. If you long for endless days filled with outdoor adventures, cultural festivals, and the chance to explore the natural world in its full glory, summer will fulfill your every wish. But if you're drawn to the quiet beauty of snow-covered landscapes, the thrill of seeing the Northern Lights, and the warmth of Scandinavian hospitality during the coziest time of year, winter will steal your heart.

Entry Requirements and Visa Information

For many travelers, visiting this enchanting region means securing a Schengen Visa, a unified visa that grants access to 27 European countries, including Denmark, Sweden, Norway, and Finland. While the process might seem daunting at first, with a bit of planning and the right information, you'll find it to be a straightforward and manageable part of your journey.

The first thing to determine is whether you need a visa at all. If you hold a passport from the United States, Canada, Australia, or any other country on the Schengen Visa exemption list, you're permitted to stay in Scandinavia for up to 90 days within a 180-day period without a visa. This is perfect for a short-term visit, whether you're there to marvel at the fjords of Norway, explore Sweden's historic cities, or enjoy the Northern Lights in Finnish Lapland. However, if your nationality requires a visa, or if you're planning to stay longer or for purposes such as work or study, you'll need to apply for a Schengen Visa.

Applying for a Schengen Visa involves several steps, and it's best to begin the process well in advance—ideally three months before your planned travel date. The application process starts with determining the country you'll enter first or where you'll spend the most time during your visit, as this dictates which embassy or consulate to apply through. For example, if your primary destination is Denmark, you'll apply through the Danish embassy or visa center in your country.

Once you've identified the correct embassy, it's time to gather the required documents. These typically include a completed visa application form, a valid passport with at least two blank pages and six months of validity beyond your stay, recent passport-sized photos, proof of travel insurance with a minimum coverage of €30,000, and your travel itinerary, including flight and hotel reservations. You'll also need to provide proof of sufficient funds, such as recent bank statements, to demonstrate that you can cover your expenses during your stay.

Booking your flights and accommodation in advance is crucial, not only to support your visa application but also to secure the best deals. Companies like Skyscanner and Kayak offer competitive flight options, while platforms like Booking.com and Airbnb are excellent for finding a wide range of accommodations. When booking flights, try to opt for flexible tickets in case you need to adjust your plans. Most major airlines, including SAS (Scandinavian Airlines), Finnair, and Norwegian, offer routes to Scandinavia's main airports in Copenhagen, Oslo, Stockholm, and Helsinki.

The visa application fee varies depending on your age and nationality, but for most travelers, it's €80 for adults and €40 for children aged 6-12. Children under six and certain other categories, such as researchers and students attending academic programs, may be exempt from fees. Payments are usually made during your visa appointment, and some embassies accept only specific methods, such as card payments or direct bank transfers. It's wise to check the payment details on the website of the embassy or visa center where you'll apply.

Once you've prepared your documents, you'll schedule an appointment at the designated embassy, consulate, or visa application center. During this appointment, you'll submit your application, provide biometric data (fingerprints and a photo), and may be asked a few questions about your trip. The process typically takes about 15-20 minutes, and afterward, you'll receive a receipt with a tracking number to monitor your application status.

Processing times for Schengen Visas vary but generally range from 15 to 30 days. To avoid delays, ensure your application is complete and accurate. Once approved, your visa will be affixed to your passport, and you'll be ready to explore Scandinavia! Remember to double-check the visa's validity dates and the number of entries permitted, as this information is crucial for planning your trip.

Beyond the visa process, it's essential to familiarize yourself with customs regulations and duty-free allowances when entering Scandinavia. Each country has its own rules, but as members of the European Union (except for Norway, which has separate guidelines), the allowances are generally similar. Travelers can bring in up to 1 liter of spirits, 4 liters of wine, and 16 liters of beer duty-free, along with 200 cigarettes or 250 grams of other tobacco products. It's important to note that these allowances are for personal use only and cannot be sold or transferred.

If you're carrying any goods that exceed these limits, you'll need to declare them upon arrival and pay the applicable duties. Additionally, there are restrictions on certain items, such as weapons, counterfeit goods, and large amounts of cash exceeding €10,000, which must also be declared. Customs officers in Scandinavia are professional and efficient, so as long as you follow the rules, the process is typically quick and hassle-free.

One thing to keep in mind is that Norway, while part of the Schengen Zone, is not a member of the EU. This means that its customs regulations differ slightly from those of Denmark, Sweden, and Finland. For example, Norway has stricter limits on bringing in meat and dairy products, so it's worth checking their specific guidelines if your itinerary includes this country.

To make your entry into Scandinavia as smooth as possible, consider arriving during non-peak hours and at major airports, which are well-equipped to handle international travelers. Copenhagen Airport, Oslo Gardermoen, Stockholm Arlanda, and Helsinki-Vantaa are all modern and efficient, offering seamless immigration and customs procedures. Having your documents organized and easily accessible can save time and reduce stress, ensuring a pleasant start to your journey. Travel insurance is another essential consideration. While it's a requirement for obtaining a Schengen Visa, it's also a practical safeguard. Scandinavia is known for its high-quality healthcare, but medical costs can be significant for uninsured travelers. Policies from companies like Allianz, AXA, or World Nomads provide comprehensive coverage for medical emergencies, trip cancellations, and lost luggage, giving you peace of mind as you explore the region.

Getting to Scandinavia

The major international airports in Scandinavia—Copenhagen Airport (CPH), Stockholm Arlanda Airport (ARN), Oslo Gardermoen Airport (OSL), Helsinki-Vantaa Airport (HEL), and Keflavik International Airport (KEF) in Reykjavik—serve as the primary gateways to the region. Each airport is modern, efficient, and equipped to handle millions of passengers annually. Copenhagen Airport, for instance, is not only Denmark's busiest airport but also a key hub for Scandinavian Airlines (SAS), offering extensive connectivity across Europe and beyond. Stockholm Arlanda is Sweden's largest airport, boasting direct flights to over 180 destinations worldwide. Meanwhile, Oslo Gardermoen provides a warm welcome to travelers with its award-winning design and commitment to sustainability, and Helsinki-Vantaa is celebrated for its efficiency and passenger-friendly amenities. Keflavik, located about 50 kilometers from Reykjavik, is Iceland's main international gateway and is especially popular for transatlantic layovers.

For travelers coming from North America, direct flights to Scandinavia are plentiful. Scandinavian Airlines (SAS), Finnair, and Icelandair are among the top carriers offering convenient routes. SAS operates direct flights from major cities such as New York (JFK),

Chicago (ORD), and Los Angeles (LAX) to Copenhagen, Stockholm, and Oslo. Finnair connects North America to Helsinki with direct flights from cities like New York and Miami, while Icelandair offers the unique option of a layover in Reykjavik at no additional cost, allowing you to explore Iceland on your way to Scandinavia. Prices for round-trip tickets from North America typically range between $500 and $1,200, depending on the season, booking time, and class of travel. For instance, booking a flight from New York to Copenhagen with SAS might cost around $650 if booked three months in advance, while a similar flight in peak summer months could exceed $1,000.

Europe, being geographically closer, offers even more flight options. Budget airlines like Ryanair, easyJet, and Wizz Air provide frequent and affordable services to Scandinavia from cities across the continent. For example, a flight from London Stansted to Stockholm with Ryanair might cost as little as €30 for a one-way ticket, though additional fees for baggage and seat selection can add up. Full-service carriers such as Lufthansa, British Airways, and Air France also offer regular flights to Scandinavian capitals, often including checked baggage and inflight meals. A round-trip ticket from Paris to Helsinki on Finnair, for instance, might cost around €250 during shoulder seasons like spring or autumn.

Travelers from Asia also have numerous options for reaching Scandinavia. Finnair is particularly notable for its extensive network in Asia, offering direct flights from cities like Tokyo, Shanghai, and Delhi to Helsinki. Known for its geographically advantageous location, Helsinki serves as a convenient stopover for Asian travelers heading to other Scandinavian destinations. Singapore Airlines and Thai Airways also provide direct flights to Copenhagen, while Japan Airlines connects Tokyo to Stockholm. Ticket prices from Asia generally range from $700 to $1,500 for economy class, with business class options offering greater comfort for longer journeys.

If you prefer a slower, more scenic route, ferries are a fantastic way to reach Scandinavia. Several operators offer services from the UK and Continental Europe, allowing you to enjoy the journey as much as the destination. From the UK, DFDS Seaways runs a popular overnight ferry from Newcastle to Amsterdam, where you can easily connect to Scandinavia by train or short flight. Prices for this route start at around £100 per person for a cabin and go up depending on amenities and class of travel. Another option is the Color Line ferry, which operates routes from Kiel, Germany, to Oslo, Norway. This luxurious ferry features restaurants, shops, and even a spa, making the 20-hour journey an experience in itself. Tickets start at approximately €150 per person, with car transportation available for an additional fee.

For travelers coming from Continental Europe, ferries are even more convenient. Stena Line offers routes from Kiel to Gothenburg, Sweden, and from Frederikshavn, Denmark, to Oslo. These crossings are particularly appealing for those looking to explore Scandinavia by car, as they allow you to bring your vehicle onboard. Prices for ferry tickets typically range from €50 to €200, depending on the route, time of year, and whether you're traveling with a car. Baltic Sea ferries like Tallink Silja and Viking Line are also popular, connecting cities such as Helsinki, Stockholm, and Tallinn, Estonia. These routes are great for short regional hops and often include entertainment and dining options onboard.

Booking your journey to Scandinavia is easier than ever, thanks to the abundance of online platforms. Websites like Skyscanner and Google Flights allow you to compare airfares across multiple airlines and find the best deals. For ferry bookings, Direct Ferries and the official websites of operators like DFDS Seaways and Stena Line are reliable options. When making your reservations, it's always a good idea to choose flexible tickets if your plans are subject to change. Many airlines and ferry companies now offer free or low-cost changes, giving you peace of mind as you finalize your itinerary.

Once your travel is booked, you'll receive a booking confirmation with all the essential details, including your ticket number, travel dates, and check-in requirements. For example, if you've booked a flight with SAS from New York to Stockholm, your ticket might display a booking number like "SK1234" and instruct you to check in online 24 hours before departure. Similarly, a ferry ticket from Kiel to Oslo with Color Line will include your cabin details, vehicle registration (if applicable), and embarkation times.

Budgeting for Your Trip

Accommodation is one of the largest expenses for any trip, and Scandinavia offers a wide range of options to fit different budgets. For budget travelers, hostels and budget hotels are the way to go. In cities like Copenhagen, Stockholm, and Oslo, you can find hostels like Generator Copenhagen or City Backpackers in Stockholm offering dorm beds for around $30–$50 per night. If privacy is a priority, some budget hotels like Cabinn in Denmark or Comfort Hotels in Norway provide small but functional private rooms starting at $80 per night. For those traveling on a mid-range budget, boutique hotels and well-rated chain hotels such as Scandic or Thon Hotels are excellent choices, with prices typically ranging from $150 to $250 per night. These properties often include breakfast, which is a huge plus in an otherwise pricey dining environment. Luxury travelers will find no shortage of opulent options, from the grand Hotel d'Angleterre in Copenhagen to the Arctic TreeHouse Hotel in Finnish Lapland, where prices can range from $400 to well over $1,000 per night, offering unparalleled service, design, and amenities.

Dining is another essential consideration when planning your budget. Scandinavia is known for its exceptional food, but eating out can be expensive. For those on a tight budget, street food markets, bakeries, and grocery stores are your best friends. A quick meal, like a hot dog from a stand in Copenhagen or a freshly baked cinnamon bun from a Swedish café, costs around $5–$10. Many grocery stores like Coop, ICA, and Rema 1000 offer ready-to-eat meals for under $10, which is a lifesaver for budget-conscious travelers. Mid-range dining options typically include casual restaurants and gastropubs, where a meal might cost $20–$40 per person. Be sure to try traditional dishes like Swedish meatballs, Danish smørrebrød, or Norwegian salmon. For luxury dining, Scandinavia is home to some of the world's best restaurants, including Copenhagen's Noma, where tasting menus can exceed $400 per person. These experiences are a splurge but offer a deep dive into the region's culinary creativity and use of local ingredients.

Activities and sightseeing in Scandinavia vary widely in cost, depending on your interests. Many of the region's natural attractions, such as hiking trails in Norway or swimming in Sweden's archipelagos, are completely free. Museums and cultural sites in cities often charge admission fees ranging from $10 to $25. However, investing in city passes like the Copenhagen Card, Stockholm Pass, or Oslo Pass can save you money if you plan to visit multiple attractions. For example, the Copenhagen Card costs approximately $65 for 24 hours and includes entry to over 80 attractions as well as unlimited public transportation. Adventure seekers might want to budget for unique experiences like dog sledding in Lapland or cruising through Norway's fjords. These activities typically cost between $150 and $500, but they are often highlights of a trip to Scandinavia.

Transportation costs can add up quickly, but there are ways to save. Scandinavia's public transport systems are world-class, and getting around by bus, train, or metro is efficient and reliable. For budget travelers, purchasing travel passes can make a big difference. In Stockholm, a 7-day travel card costs around $40 and provides unlimited rides on public transport, while Copenhagen's city zones offer similar options starting at $12 for a 24-hour ticket. If you're planning to travel between cities or countries, trains are a comfortable and scenic choice. While individual tickets can be expensive—such as $60 for a one-way trip between Oslo and Gothenburg—booking in advance or using discount cards like the Eurail Scandinavia Pass can save you up to 30%. For example, a 3-day pass valid across Denmark, Sweden, Norway, and Finland starts at around $230, allowing flexible travel over a month.

Ferries are another iconic way to explore Scandinavia, especially its many islands and coastal routes. Companies like Viking Line and Tallink Silja operate affordable routes between Stockholm, Helsinki, and Tallinn, with tickets starting at $20 for a basic seat. These ferries often double as floating hotels, with cabins available for those who prefer a more comfortable overnight journey. Budget-conscious travelers can often find deals on these routes, especially if booking mid-week or off-season.

Money-saving tips can stretch your budget even further. One effective strategy is to travel during the shoulder seasons—spring and autumn—when accommodations and flights are significantly cheaper, and crowds are thinner. Additionally, Scandinavia is incredibly friendly to outdoor enthusiasts, and many of its best attractions—like hiking in Norway's fjords or exploring Denmark's beaches—are free or low-cost. Another tip is to take advantage of free or donation-based walking tours available in major cities. These tours are not only budget-friendly but also offer a fantastic way to learn about local history and culture from passionate guides.

For everyday expenses, it's worth noting that Scandinavia is almost entirely cashless. Credit and debit cards are widely accepted, even for small purchases, so you won't need to carry much cash. Some banks charge foreign transaction fees, so using a travel-friendly card without fees can help you save.

Planning your trip with a clear budget in mind allows you to tailor your experience without feeling restricted. For a weeklong trip, a budget traveler might spend around $1,000–$1,500, covering hostels, groceries, and free activities. A mid-range traveler could budget $2,500–$3,500, including boutique accommodations, casual dining, and a few paid attractions. Luxury travelers can expect to spend $5,000 or more, indulging in high-end hotels, fine dining, and exclusive experiences.

Packing Guide

If you're visiting Scandinavia in the winter, you'll need to prioritize warmth and layering. Temperatures can drop dramatically, especially in northern regions like Lapland, where the mercury often plunges well below freezing. A good-quality insulated jacket is your best friend, ideally one that's windproof and water-resistant. Underneath, layer up with thermal tops, a fleece or wool sweater, and moisture-wicking base layers. Merino wool is a fantastic choice for keeping warm without feeling bulky. Don't forget insulated, waterproof pants to protect you from snow and icy winds.

For winter adventures like dog sledding, snowshoeing, or chasing the Northern Lights, additional gear is essential. A pair of insulated, waterproof boots with good traction is nonnegotiable, as you'll likely be walking on snow and ice. Wool socks are a must, and packing a few extra pairs will save you if they get wet. Gloves, a snug hat that covers your ears, and a scarf or neck gaiter will help keep extremities warm. Many travelers also swear by hand and foot warmers, which are small, inexpensive, and lifesavers on particularly cold days. If you're heading to the Arctic Circle, consider bringing ski goggles to protect your eyes from glare and wind during outdoor activities.

In summer, Scandinavia transforms into a haven of greenery and long days, with temperatures generally ranging between 15°C and 25°C (59°F to 77°F). Packing for summer is lighter but no less thoughtful. A mix of short-sleeve shirts, lightweight long-sleeve tops, and comfortable pants or shorts is ideal. The weather can change quickly, so a packable waterproof jacket is essential, even in July. Layers are still your best bet, as mornings and evenings can be chilly, especially in the mountains or along the coast. Comfortable walking shoes or hiking boots are a must for exploring cities, trails, and rocky terrain, while sandals or slip-ons are great for casual outings.

For outdoor enthusiasts planning activities like hiking in Norway's fjords or kayaking through Sweden's archipelagos, having the right gear makes all the difference. A small daypack is invaluable for carrying essentials like water, snacks, and sunscreen during excursions. Speaking of sunscreen, don't underestimate the Scandinavian sun, especially during the summer months when daylight stretches for almost 24 hours in the northern regions. A hat and sunglasses are also recommended to protect against glare.

Regardless of the season, there are a few must-have items to include in your bag. Scandinavia's power outlets use a Type C or Type F plug, so you'll need a suitable electrical adapter if you're coming from outside Europe. If you plan to charge multiple devices, consider bringing a universal adapter with USB ports for added convenience. Additionally, a portable power bank can be a lifesaver, especially when you're out exploring all day.

Staying connected is important, and Scandinavia makes it easy with reliable mobile networks and SIM card options. If your phone is unlocked, picking up a local prepaid SIM card can save you money on data and calls. Providers like Telia, Telenor, and Elisa offer SIM cards with generous data plans, often starting at around $15 for a few gigabytes, depending on the country. These are widely available at airports, convenience stores, and kiosks. Alternatively, if you prefer to stick with your current provider, check their international roaming rates to avoid unexpected charges.

When it comes to packing toiletries, keep in mind that many Scandinavian hotels, hostels, and even some rentals provide basic amenities like shampoo and soap. This can save you space and weight in your luggage. However, if you have specific products you prefer, pack them in travel-sized containers to comply with airline regulations. Scandinavia's water is among the cleanest in the world, so a reusable water bottle is not only eco-friendly but also incredibly practical.

One item many travelers forget but find indispensable in Scandinavia is a good travel umbrella or compact rain poncho. Rain can be frequent, especially in coastal areas like Bergen, known as one of Europe's rainiest cities. It's worth investing in a sturdy, wind-resistant umbrella to avoid dealing with flimsy ones that turn inside out at the first gust

If you're someone who likes to capture memories, don't forget your camera or smartphone, along with extra memory cards and chargers. Scandinavia's landscapes are incredibly photogenic, from the dramatic cliffs of Norway's Geirangerfjord to the pastel-colored houses of Stockholm's Gamla Stan. A lightweight tripod can be a great addition if you're planning to photograph the Northern Lights or other low-light scenes. For those traveling in winter, keeping batteries warm is crucial, as cold temperatures can drain them quickly.

Finally, think about the little extras that will make your trip more enjoyable. A good book, travel journal, or e-reader is perfect for downtime during long train rides or ferry crossings. If you're planning to visit museums or attractions, consider packing a lightweight tote bag or foldable backpack for carrying souvenirs or snacks during the day.

Health and Safety Considerations

Before traveling to Scandinavia, it's important to review your vaccination records to ensure they are up to date. While there are no mandatory vaccinations for entry into these

countries, it is strongly recommended to be up to date on routine immunizations like measles, mumps, rubella (MMR), tetanus, diphtheria, and polio. Additionally, vaccines for hepatitis A and B are advisable, particularly if you plan to enjoy outdoor activities or explore rural areas where access to medical care may be limited. For travelers venturing into forested regions, especially in Sweden or Finland, a tick-borne encephalitis (TBE) vaccine is worth considering. TBE is transmitted through tick bites, and while the risk is low, it's always better to err on the side of caution. Vaccines should ideally be scheduled six to eight weeks before your trip, as some require multiple doses.

Travel insurance is another critical component of your preparations. Scandinavia's healthcare systems are world-class, but medical expenses for non-residents can be steep. An unexpected illness or injury could cost thousands without insurance, so securing a comprehensive travel insurance plan is essential. Companies like World Nomads, Allianz, and AXA offer policies tailored to international travelers, covering everything from medical emergencies to trip cancellations and lost luggage. A standard plan typically costs between $50 and $150 for a two-week trip, depending on your age, destination, and coverage level. For adventure seekers planning activities like skiing or dog sledding, be sure to select a policy that includes coverage for high-risk sports.

Knowing the emergency contact numbers in each Scandinavian country can make all the difference in an urgent situation. Dialing 112 connects you to emergency services across all Scandinavian countries, including Denmark, Sweden, Norway, Finland, and Iceland. This single number ensures access to police, ambulance, and fire services. For non-urgent medical situations, Denmark's medical hotline can be reached at +45 1813, while Sweden offers a similar service at +46 1177. In Norway, the medical helpline is +47 116 117, and Finland has +358 116 117 for health-related advice. Iceland's health hotline, reachable at +354 1700, provides 24/7 assistance. These numbers are lifesavers for situations that don't warrant an emergency room visit but still require professional guidance.

While Scandinavia is considered one of the safest regions in the world, it's always wise to take personal safety precautions. Petty crime, such as pickpocketing, is rare but can occur in crowded tourist areas or public transport hubs, especially in larger cities like Copenhagen and Stockholm. Keep your valuables secure, preferably in a money belt or an anti-theft backpack with locking zippers. Avoid carrying large amounts of cash; credit and debit cards are widely accepted, even for small transactions. If you're using ATMs, opt for those inside banks or shopping centers to minimize the risk of card skimming.

Another practical safety tip is to stay vigilant in unfamiliar surroundings, especially at night. Scandinavian cities are generally well-lit and have a low crime rate, but sticking to main streets and avoiding isolated areas is always a good idea. Public transport, including buses, trains, and ferries, is safe and reliable, even late at night. Taxis and ride-sharing services like Uber are also secure options, but if you choose to hail a cab, ensure it's from a licensed company.

For outdoor enthusiasts, Scandinavia's breathtaking wilderness is a major draw, but it comes with its own set of safety considerations. Weather can change rapidly, especially in mountainous regions or along the coast. Always check the forecast before heading out, and dress in layers to accommodate sudden temperature drops or rain. If you're planning a hike, make sure to inform someone of your route and expected return time, especially if you're exploring remote areas. Carrying a map, compass, and fully charged phone with a portable power bank is essential, as some areas may have limited cellular coverage.

When it comes to driving in Scandinavia, the well-maintained roads and courteous drivers make it a pleasure. However, certain precautions are necessary. Winter driving, particularly in Norway and Iceland, can be challenging due to snow and ice. Renting a car with winter tires and practicing defensive driving will help ensure your safety. In Iceland, be cautious on gravel roads and watch for sudden changes in weather. Renting a car from reputable companies like Hertz, Avis, or Sixt ensures reliability, with prices starting around $50 per day for a compact vehicle. Be aware that gas prices in Scandinavia are higher than the global average, often exceeding $7 per gallon, so budget accordingly.

Scandinavia's natural beauty also means encounters with wildlife are possible. If you're camping or hiking in areas known for bears, wolves, or moose, follow local guidelines to minimize risks. In Sweden, for example, keeping food stored securely and making noise while hiking can help deter wildlife. While animal encounters are rare, being prepared ensures your safety and theirs.

Staying healthy while traveling is equally important, and Scandinavia offers some of the cleanest drinking water in the world. Carry a reusable water bottle to refill as needed, saving money and reducing plastic waste. If you're sensitive to dietary changes, opt for simple, fresh foods readily available in Scandinavian cuisine, such as salmon, rye bread, and berries. Grocery stores offer a variety of options, including organic and allergen-free products, ensuring you can maintain your dietary preferences.

MUST-SEE ATTRACTIONS AND LANDMARKS

Denmark

Denmark, a country that blends rich history with modern innovation, is a true gem in Scandinavia. It's a place that feels effortlessly charming, where cobblestone streets lead to castles, vibrant harbors, and attractions that transport you through centuries of stories and traditions. From the bustling heart of Copenhagen to the serene northern coastlines of Skagen, Denmark offers experiences that are as varied as they are unforgettable. Exploring its highlights feels like stepping into a storybook, with each chapter revealing a new wonder.

Start your journey in **Copenhagen**, where **Tivoli Gardens** steals the spotlight. Located at Vesterbrogade 3, just a short walk from the city's central train station, Tivoli isn't just an amusement park—it's a cultural treasure. Opened in 1843, this enchanting space inspired Walt Disney himself. During summer, the gardens come alive with concerts, lush flower displays, and thrilling rides. In winter, it transforms into a magical wonderland with twinkling lights and festive markets. Whether you're soaring high on the Star Flyer or savoring Danish treats like æbleskiver, Tivoli captures the heart of everyone who visits.

A stroll from Tivoli brings you to one of Denmark's most iconic landmarks: The Little Mermaid. Perched on a rock at Langelinie

Promenade, this bronze statue is more than a photo opportunity—it's a tribute to Hans Christian Andersen, whose fairy tales have enchanted generations. Though the statue itself is small, the symbolism is immense. As you stand there, watching her gaze longingly out to sea, you can't help but feel connected to the timeless story of love and sacrifice. Getting there is easy, with buses and boats frequently stopping near the harbor.

Nearby, *Nyhavn* awaits with its postcard-perfect charm. Originally a bustling port in the 17th century, today this colorful harbor is a haven for travelers and locals alike. The brightly painted buildings that line the canal house cozy restaurants, pubs, and cafes. Sit by the water with a smørrebrød—a traditional Danish open-faced sandwich—and let the hum of the lively atmosphere surround you. In warmer months, wooden boats bob gently on the water, their reflections dancing alongside the canal. Nyhavn was once home to Hans Christian Andersen himself, and as you wander its cobblestone streets, it's easy to imagine the inspiration he drew from this vibrant spot.

Not far from Nyhavn, **Christiansborg** Palace stands as a testament to Denmark's royal and political history. Situated on the islet of Slotsholmen, the palace is the seat of the Danish Parliament, the Supreme Court, and the Prime Minister's Office. Its location makes it easy to reach by metro, bus, or even a leisurely walk from central Copenhagen. Touring the palace is like peeling back layers of Danish history, from the stunning Royal Reception Rooms to the underground ruins of the original castle built in the 12th century. Don't miss the chance to climb the tower for panoramic views of the city—it's free and offers a breathtaking perspective of Copenhagen's skyline.

Venturing outside the city, **Kronborg Castle**, famously known as Elsinore in Shakespeare's ***Hamlet***, is a must-visit. Located at Kronborg 2C in Helsingør, about an hour by train from Copenhagen, this UNESCO World Heritage site is a masterpiece of Renaissance architecture. As you wander its grand halls and ramparts overlooking the Øresund Strait, it's easy to imagine the intrigue and drama that inspired the Bard's most famous tragedy. The castle often hosts events and performances, making it feel alive with history and culture. Whether you're exploring the eerie underground casemates or taking in the sweeping views from the towers, Kronborg is an unforgettable experience.

For a playful twist on Danish heritage, **LEGO House** in Billund offers endless fun. Situated at Ole Kirks Vej 1, the birthplace of LEGO, this interactive attraction celebrates creativity and imagination. Getting there is simple, with direct flights to Billund Airport or train connections from major cities. Inside, the experience is hands-on and immersive. Build your own LEGO creations, explore exhibitions showcasing incredible designs, or delve into the history of the world's most famous building blocks. Perfect for families and adults alike, LEGO House sparks joy and creativity at every turn.

Denmark's natural beauty shines brightest in **Skagen**, where the coastline offers a serene escape. At the northernmost tip of the country, where the Skagerrak and Kattegat seas meet, you'll find a place unlike any other. Grenen, the sandy spit where the two seas collide, is a spectacle of nature. The best way to get there is by car or bus, with the journey offering scenic views of the Danish countryside. Skagen itself is a quaint town with a rich artistic legacy. The Skagen Painters, a group of 19th-century artists, were drawn to the unique light of this region, and their works are celebrated at the Skagens Museum. Walking along the windswept beaches or enjoying fresh seafood at a local eatery, you'll feel the peaceful magic that makes Skagen so special.

Timing your visit to Denmark can enhance your experience. Summer, from June to August, offers the most pleasant weather, with long days perfect for outdoor adventures. This is the ideal time to enjoy Tivoli's concerts,

Nyhavn's bustling cafes, and the beaches of Skagen. However, winter brings its own kind of charm. From November to December, Denmark's cities light up with Christmas markets, and Tivoli becomes a winter wonderland. Spring and autumn are quieter but equally enchanting, offering mild weather and fewer crowds.

Sweden

Sweden is a land of contrasts, where vibrant cities meet serene wilderness, and centuries-old traditions blend seamlessly with modern innovation. It's a place that captivates with its charm, from the cobblestone streets of Stockholm's Gamla Stan to the untouched beauty of Lapland. Exploring Sweden feels like flipping through a travelogue filled with culture, history, and natural wonders. Whether you're drawn to iconic museums, stunning architecture, or the call of the Arctic wilderness, Sweden offers a tapestry of experiences that leaves every traveler enchanted.

Begin your journey in Stockholm, the beating heart of Sweden and a city spread across 14 islands. **Gamla Stan**, the city's Old Town, is like stepping back in time. As you wander the narrow, winding streets lined with colorful medieval buildings, it's easy to imagine the history that has unfolded here since its founding in 1252. Stortorget Square, the picturesque centerpiece of Gamla Stan, is surrounded by vibrant facades and bustling cafes. You'll find treasures around every corner, from the majestic Stockholm Cathedral to the Royal Palace, one of Europe's largest palaces still in use by a monarchy. The area is easily accessible by metro to Gamla Stan station or a short walk from central Stockholm, and the charm of its cobblestone streets is an experience you won't forget.

Not far from Gamla Stan lies the **Vasa Museum**, a must-visit for history enthusiasts and curious travelers alike.

Located on the island of Djurgården at Galärvarvsvägen 14, this museum is home to the Vasa, a 17th-century warship that sank on its maiden voyage and was salvaged more than 300 years later. Walking into the museum feels like stepping into another era, as the massive, almost entirely intact ship looms before you. Guided tours and interactive exhibits bring the Vasa's story to life, offering a glimpse into Sweden's maritime history. Getting to the museum is simple, with buses and trams stopping nearby, and the experience is well worth the 190 SEK admission fee.

For something completely different but equally captivating, the *ABBA Museum* is a joyful celebration of Sweden's most famous musical export. Located at Djurgårdsvägen 68 on the same island as the Vasa Museum, this interactive attraction is a must for fans of the legendary pop group. From original costumes to memorabilia and immersive exhibits, the museum lets you step into the world of ABBA like never before. You can even record your own version of their hits or virtually join them on stage. Tickets are priced at 250 SEK, and booking online in advance is recommended, especially during peak travel seasons. The energy and nostalgia of the ABBA Museum make it an experience that transcends generations, even if you weren't alive during the band's heyday.

Heading north, the *Icehotel in Jukkasjärvi* is a bucket-list destination that combines art, architecture, and the sheer beauty of the Arctic. Located 200 kilometers above the Arctic Circle, this world-famous hotel is rebuilt every winter entirely from ice and snow harvested from the nearby Torne River. Each suite is uniquely designed by artists, making every stay a one-of-a-kind experience. The best way to reach the Icehotel is by flying into Kiruna Airport and taking a short 15-minute transfer to Jukkasjärvi. While staying overnight in an ice suite is a once-in-a-lifetime experience, day visitors can also tour the hotel, admire its stunning ice sculptures, and even enjoy a drink in the Ice Bar. The best time to visit is between December and April, when the hotel is fully constructed and the Northern Lights frequently illuminate the night sky.

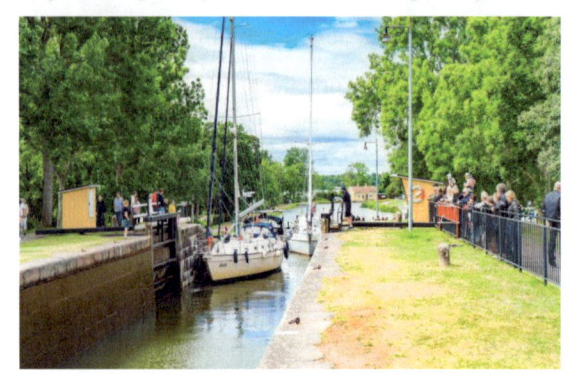

For a more relaxed and scenic experience, the **Göta Canal** offers a glimpse into Sweden's engineering ingenuity and natural beauty. Stretching over 190 kilometers and connecting the east and west coasts, the canal passes through picturesque landscapes, charming villages, and more than 50 locks. One of the best ways to experience it is aboard a canal cruise, with operators like Göta Kanal Rederi offering multi-day journeys. Cruises typically depart from Gothenburg or Stockholm, and prices range from 10,000 SEK for a two-day trip to 35,000 SEK for a six-day luxury cruise. Alternatively, you can rent a bike or kayak and explore the canal at your own pace, soaking in the tranquility of the Swedish countryside.

Venturing into the far north, **Swedish Lapland** is a realm of rugged beauty and deep cultural roots. This is where the indigenous Sami people have lived for generations, maintaining their traditions and connection to the land. Visiting a Sami village is a deeply enriching experience, offering insight into their way of life, reindeer herding practices, and unique crafts. Jokkmokk, the heart of Sami culture, hosts an annual winter market that has been held for over 400 years. Getting to Lapland typically involves a flight to Kiruna or Luleå, followed by a train or bus ride to your destination. The best time to visit is during the winter months, when you can pair your cultural exploration with thrilling activities like dog sledding, snowmobiling, or simply marveling at the Northern Lights.

Sweden's seasons bring different experiences, each worth embracing. Summer, from June to August, offers long days filled with sunshine and opportunities to explore the country's lakes, forests, and islands. The Midnight Sun in the northern regions is a phenomenon that must be seen to be believed. In contrast, winter transforms the landscape into a snowy wonderland, perfect for skiing, snowshoeing, and cozy evenings by the fire. Spring and autumn are quieter but equally beautiful, with blossoming flowers or fiery foliage adding a touch of magic to the scenery.

Getting around Sweden is a breeze, thanks to its efficient and reliable public transport system. The high-speed SJ trains connect major cities like Stockholm, Gothenburg, and Malmö, while regional buses and ferries make reaching smaller towns and islands easy. If you plan to explore extensively, consider purchasing a travel pass, such as the Interrail Sweden Pass, which offers unlimited train travel for a set number of days.

Norway

Norway is a place that feels like stepping into a storybook, where every turn reveals a dramatic fjord, a historic landmark, or a natural wonder that takes your breath away. Whether you're standing on the edge of a cliff, marveling at a Viking ship, or riding one of the world's most scenic railways, Norway offers experiences that linger in your heart long after you've left. It's a country that blends nature's raw power with rich cultural heritage, making it one of Scandinavia's most captivating destinations.

Bergen is often the starting point for exploring Norway's iconic fjords, and it's not hard to see why. This charming coastal city, surrounded by seven mountains, is a living postcard. Its historic Bryggen Wharf, a UNESCO World Heritage Site, is lined with colorful wooden buildings that once housed traders in the Hanseatic League. Today, they're home to boutique shops, art galleries, and cozy cafes. Wandering through its narrow alleyways feels like stepping back in time. Bergen is also the gateway to the fjords, with countless tours departing from the harbor. Don't miss a cruise through the Sognefjord, Norway's longest and deepest fjord, where towering cliffs and cascading waterfalls create an unforgettable landscape. Getting to Bergen is simple, with direct flights from major European cities or a scenic seven-hour train ride from Oslo.

Speaking of Oslo, the capital city offers a perfect mix of modernity and tradition. The **Oslo Opera House,** located at Kirsten Flagstads Plass 1, is a striking piece of contemporary architecture that appears to rise from the waters of the Oslofjord. Its sloping roof is open to the public, allowing you to walk to the top for panoramic views of the city and fjord. Inside, world-class performances range from opera to ballet, but even if you're not attending a show, the building itself is worth a visit. Tickets for performances vary but often start around 300 NOK. From the Opera House, a short bus or ferry ride takes you to the Viking Ship Museum at Huk Aveny 35. This museum is home to beautifully preserved ships from the Viking Age, including the Oseberg and Gokstad ships, which are over 1,000 years old. Walking around these masterpieces of craftsmanship gives you a deep appreciation for the seafaring legacy of the Vikings.

For a truly otherworldly experience, head north to the **Lofoten Islands.** Known for their jagged peaks, pristine beaches, and fishing villages, the islands feel like a slice of Arctic paradise. The best way to get there is by flying into Bodø and taking a ferry to Svolvær, the main town. Once on the islands, rent a car to explore at your own pace. Drive along winding roads that hug the coastline, stopping to admire turquoise bays and red-and-white rorbu cabins perched on stilts. Activities abound, from kayaking under the Midnight Sun in summer to chasing the Northern Lights in winter. Don't miss a visit to the charming village of Reine, where the dramatic landscape is so stunning it's often featured in travel brochures. Lofoten is also a hiker's paradise, with trails like Reinebringen offering views that are worth every step.

For adventurers seeking thrills, Norway's cliffs and plateaus provide some of the most iconic hiking experiences in the world. Pulpit Rock, or Preikestolen, is one of the country's most famous landmarks. Located near Stavanger, it's a sheer cliff that rises 604 meters above Lysefjord. The four-hour round-trip hike is accessible to most fitness levels, and the reward at the top is a jaw-dropping view of the fjord stretching into the distance. Slightly more challenging is Trolltunga, a rock formation that juts out like a tongue above Lake Ringedalsvatnet. This hike, near Odda, is a full-day adventure covering 28 kilometers, but the feeling of standing on the edge, with the world seemingly at your feet, is indescribable. Both trails are best tackled in summer, from June to September, when conditions are safer and the weather is more predictable.

For a change of pace, the **Flåm Railway** offers one of the most scenic train journeys on the planet. This 20-kilometer route connects the small village of Flåm, nestled at the end of Aurlandsfjord, with the mountain station of Myrdal. The train climbs nearly 900 meters, passing through dramatic landscapes of waterfalls, deep ravines, and snow-capped peaks. One of the highlights is Kjosfossen Waterfall, where the train makes a brief stop, allowing you to step out and feel the mist on your face. Tickets for the Flåm Railway start at around 450 NOK for a one-way trip and can be booked online or at the station. Pair this journey with a cruise on the fjord for an unforgettable day.

Norway's beauty reaches its peak in its natural wonders, but it's the seamless blending of these with cultural experiences that makes the country so special. Every region offers something unique, and the time of year can shape your experience. Summer, from June to August, is ideal for hiking, fjord cruises, and experiencing the Midnight Sun. Winter, from November to March, transforms the landscape into a snowy wonderland perfect for Northern Lights hunting, dog sledding, and skiing. Spring and autumn are quieter, offering a chance to see the changing seasons without the crowds.

Traveling through Norway is as much a pleasure as the destinations themselves. The country's trains, buses, and ferries are efficient and offer stunning views along the way. If you're planning to cover multiple regions, consider the Norway in a Nutshell tour, a customizable journey that includes the Flåm Railway, fjord cruises, and scenic bus rides. Prices start at around 1,600 NOK and are worth every penny for the convenience and beauty of the route.

Finland

Finland is a destination that surprises and delights at every turn. Whether you're wandering through Helsinki's vibrant streets, marveling at the natural beauty of its countless lakes, or basking under the Midnight Sun in the Arctic Circle, this Nordic gem offers an experience that feels both deeply personal and profoundly unique. Finland's attractions range from urban sophistication to untouched wilderness, blending modern innovation with ancient traditions that make every visit unforgettable.

Start your Finnish adventure in **Helsinki**, a city where design and creativity are woven into its very fabric. The Design District, located in the heart of the city, is a testament to Finland's reputation for world-class design. Spanning the neighborhoods of Punavuori, Ullanlinna, and Kaartinkaupunki, this area is home to over 200 design studios, galleries, boutiques, and cafes. Walking through its streets feels like stepping into a living art gallery, with every storefront showcasing minimalist furniture, handcrafted jewelry, or innovative home goods. Marimekko, one of Finland's most iconic design brands, has a flagship store here that's a must-visit. The district is easily reached by tram or on foot, and it's the perfect place to pick up unique souvenirs or simply soak in the creative atmosphere. If you're a lover of architecture, don't miss the nearby Kamppi Chapel of Silence, a stunning wooden structure that offers a peaceful retreat amidst the city's buzz.

From Helsinki, it's a short ferry ride to **Suomenlinna Fortress,** a UNESCO World Heritage Site and one of Finland's most cherished landmarks. Located on a cluster of islands in Helsinki's harbor, Suomenlinna is an 18th-century sea fortress that once protected the city from naval invasions. Today, it's a fascinating destination where history meets natural beauty. You can explore its cobblestone paths, admire the preserved fortifications, and even visit the Suomenlinna Museum to learn about its strategic importance. The islands are also a great spot for a picnic, with views of the sea and passing boats creating a serene backdrop. Ferries to Suomenlinna run frequently from Helsinki's Market Square, with round-trip tickets costing around €5. The best time to visit is in the summer months, when the weather is warm and the lush greenery adds to the fortress's charm.

For those seeking a touch of magic, **Rovaniemi**, the capital of Finnish Lapland, is a destination that feels like stepping into a winter wonderland. Officially recognized as the hometown of Santa Claus, Rovaniemi is home to the Santa Claus Village, a place where childhood dreams come to life. Located just 8 kilometers from Rovaniemi Airport, the village is open year-round and offers the chance to meet Santa himself, send postcards from the official Santa Claus Post Office, and cross the Arctic Circle. Winter is an especially magical time to visit, with the village adorned in twinkling lights and covered in snow. Entrance to the village is free, though activities like reindeer sleigh rides or visiting Santa's private office may have additional costs.

While in **Lapland**, staying in a glass igloo is an experience that's as unforgettable as it is surreal. Resorts like Kakslauttanen Arctic Resort and Arctic SnowHotel & Glass Igloos offer the opportunity to sleep under the stars in luxury. These igloos, equipped with heated glass roofs, provide unobstructed views of the Northern Lights during winter and the Midnight Sun in summer. Prices start at around €400 per night, making it a splurge-worthy addition to your trip. Imagine lying in a warm bed while watching the Aurora Borealis dance across the sky—a memory you'll treasure forever.

Finland's natural beauty shines brightest in Finnish Lakeland, a region of over 180,000 lakes that stretches across the country's heartland. This is where you'll find tranquility and connection with nature, whether you're kayaking through crystal-clear waters, hiking through dense forests, or enjoying the traditional Finnish pastime of sauna. Rent a lakeside cabin for a few days to fully immerse yourself in the serene surroundings. Towns like Savonlinna, famous for its medieval Olavinlinna Castle, offer a perfect blend of history and natural splendor. During summer, the Savonlinna Opera Festival is a highlight, attracting performers and audiences from around the world to this picturesque lakeside setting.

The Midnight Sun is one of Finland's most extraordinary natural phenomena, offering nearly 24 hours of daylight in the summer months. The best place to experience this is in the northernmost parts of Finland, where the sun doesn't set for weeks. In Rovaniemi or further north in Utsjoki, you can take midnight hikes, go fishing, or simply sit by a campfire and marvel at the endless daylight. The Midnight Sun creates a unique energy that makes every activity feel special, as though time itself has paused to let you savor the moment.

Getting around Finland is straightforward and convenient, with excellent transport options connecting cities and remote regions alike. Helsinki serves as the main gateway, with direct flights from major European hubs and long-haul destinations like New York, Tokyo, and Singapore. Trains operated by VR provide comfortable and efficient connections across the country, including the overnight Santa Claus Express from Helsinki to Rovaniemi. If you're planning to explore multiple regions, consider renting a car for flexibility, particularly in Lakeland or Lapland.

The best time to visit Finland depends on what you want to experience. Winter, from December to March, is ideal for snowy adventures, Northern Lights viewing, and Christmas magic. Summer, from June to August, offers long, sunny days perfect for exploring lakes, islands, and outdoor festivals. Spring and autumn bring quieter crowds, with blooming flowers or vibrant foliage adding seasonal beauty to the landscape.

Iceland

Iceland is a land of unparalleled beauty, where natural wonders and vibrant culture come together in a way that feels almost otherworldly. From its dramatic glaciers and geothermal pools to its charming capital city, Iceland invites you to explore a world that's as raw as it is magical. Whether you're gazing up at the Northern Lights or soaking in the warm waters of the Blue Lagoon, every moment here feels like a gift from nature. Let me take you through some of the country's most unforgettable experiences, starting in Reykjavik and leading you to Iceland's most iconic attractions.

Reykjavik, Iceland's capital, is a city that effortlessly combines the old and the new. At its heart stands Hallgrímskirkja, a towering **Lutheran church** that is as much a symbol of the city as it is a work of art. Located at Hallgrímstorg 1, this striking structure was inspired by Iceland's basalt landscapes and volcanic formations. As you approach, the church's 74.5-meter-tall spire becomes an unmissable beacon. Inside, the minimalist design allows the massive pipe organ to take center stage—a truly awe-inspiring sight. For a small fee of about 1,200 ISK (roughly $9), you can take an elevator to the top, where panoramic views of Reykjavik and the surrounding mountains await. Whether it's your first day in the city or your last, standing at the top of Hallgrímskirkja feels like a moment of connection with the soul of Iceland.

From Reykjavik, the **Golden Circle** is an easy and essential day trip that showcases Iceland's unique geology and natural beauty. The route covers three main attractions: Thingvellir National Park, Geysir Geothermal Area, and Gullfoss Waterfall. Thingvellir, a UNESCO World Heritage Site, is where the North American and Eurasian tectonic plates meet. Walking through this rift valley, you can quite literally straddle two continents—a surreal experience that's both educational and breathtaking. The Geysir Geothermal Area, located nearby, is home to the famous Strokkur geyser, which erupts every few minutes, sending hot water shooting up to 20 meters into the air. Watching it in action is thrilling and humbling, a reminder of the Earth's raw power. The final stop, Gullfoss, is a cascading waterfall that roars with intensity as it plunges into a canyon. The entire Golden Circle route is about 300 kilometers and can be done in a day, either by renting a car or joining one of the many guided tours from Reykjavik. Tours typically cost between 10,000 and 15,000 ISK ($75–$110), and most include informative guides who add depth to the experience.

No trip to Iceland would be complete without a visit to the **Blue Lagoon,** a geothermal spa located in the Reykjanes Peninsula, just 45 minutes from Reykjavik. The lagoon's milky-blue waters, rich in minerals like silica and sulfur, are not only stunning but also incredibly soothing for the skin. It's the perfect place to unwind after exploring Iceland's rugged terrain. Admission prices vary depending on the time of year and package, starting at around 9,900 ISK ($75) for the basic Comfort package, which includes a silica mud mask, a towel, and a drink. For those seeking extra luxury, the Premium package or even a stay at the adjacent Retreat Hotel offers a more exclusive experience. Whether you're soaking in the warm waters under a soft snowfall or on a sunny day, the Blue Lagoon is an otherworldly experience you'll carry with you long after you've left.

Heading further afield, *Jökulsárlón Glacier Lagoon* is one of Iceland's most mesmerizing sights. Located along the southeastern coast, about 370 kilometers from Reykjavik, this glacial lagoon is a natural masterpiece where massive icebergs drift serenely across blue waters. The icebergs, which calve from the nearby Breiðamerkurjökull Glacier, come in shades of white, blue, and black, reflecting the interplay of light and volcanic ash trapped within the ice. Boat tours, which cost around 7,000 ISK ($50), allow you to get up close to these floating giants, and some even include the chance to taste 1,000-year-old glacial ice. Nearby Diamond Beach, where chunks of ice wash up on black sand, is a must-see and provides a striking contrast that's perfect for photography. The drive to Jökulsárlón from Reykjavik takes about five hours, but the stunning landscapes along the way make the journey part of the adventure. Alternatively, guided tours often combine the lagoon with other south coast highlights for a hassle-free experience.

One of the most magical reasons to visit Iceland is to witness the **Northern Lights, or aurora borealis.** These ethereal lights dance across the Arctic skies, painting the darkness with ribbons of green, pink, and purple. While the phenomenon is never guaranteed, Iceland's long winter nights, from September to April, offer some of the best chances to see them. Reykjavik itself has Northern Lights tours departing almost nightly during the season. These tours, which start at around 7,000 ISK ($50), take you away from the city lights to darker, more remote locations where the auroras are most visible. Some tours even offer photography tips, helping you capture the perfect shot of this fleeting natural wonder. For a truly immersive experience, consider heading to areas like Thingvellir or the Snaefellsnes Peninsula, where the unspoiled wilderness makes the lights even more dramatic. It's worth dressing warmly—thermal layers, insulated boots, and a good hat are essential for standing outside on crisp Arctic nights.

The best time to visit Iceland depends on what you want to experience. Summer, from June to August, brings long days and milder temperatures, perfect for exploring the Golden Circle and Jökulsárlón Glacier Lagoon. Winter, from November to March, offers the chance to see the Northern Lights and enjoy the cozy atmosphere of Reykjavik's cafes and cultural attractions. Spring and autumn are quieter, with fewer crowds and opportunities to witness Iceland's changing landscapes.

ACCOMMODATION OPTIONS

Luxury Hotels and Resorts

Hotel d'Angleterre, Copenhagen: Located at Kongens Nytorv 34 in the heart of Copenhagen, this iconic five-star hotel has been synonymous with luxury since 1755. The hotel features 92 exquisitely designed rooms and suites, each offering a blend of historical charm and contemporary comforts. Guests rave about the Michelin-starred restaurant, Marchal, and the award-winning Amazing Space spa. Pricing starts at 5,000 DKK ($700) per night for a deluxe room, but the experience is worth every krone. Booking is straightforward through their website or by calling +45 33 12 00 95. The prime location makes it easy to explore landmarks like Nyhavn and Tivoli Gardens. Pros include world-class service, elegant interiors, and unmatched dining. However, the cost can be prohibitive for some travelers, and availability during peak seasons is limited.

Arctic Bath, Swedish Lapland: Nestled on the Lule River in Harads, Arctic Bath is a floating spa and wellness retreat unlike any other. With six overwater cabins and six land-based suites, it offers a minimalist design inspired by Scandinavian nature. Rooms start at around 10,000 SEK ($950) per night, including breakfast and spa access. Booking can be done directly via their website or by calling +46 928 21 00 01. During the winter months, the frozen river transforms the experience into a true Arctic escape, while summer offers the Midnight Sun and kayaking opportunities. Pros include the serenity of the remote location, unique design, and exceptional spa treatments. On the downside, the remote setting requires careful planning for transportation, and activities are heavily weather-dependent.

The Thief, Oslo: Perched on the Oslofjord waterfront at Landgangen 1, The Thief is a sleek, art-focused five-star hotel that lives up to its daring name. Each room features floor-to-ceiling windows, plush furnishings, and original artwork. The hotel's rooftop bar is a highlight, offering sweeping views of the city. Rooms start at 4,500 NOK ($420) per night, and reservations can be made by calling +47 24 00 40 00 or through their website. Its proximity to the Astrup Fearnley Museum of Modern Art and the trendy Tjuvholmen neighborhood makes it a cultural hub. Guests appreciate the attentive service, cutting-edge amenities, and excellent dining options. The cons? The contemporary style may feel impersonal to those seeking a more traditional luxury experience, and prices can spike during high demand periods.

Kakslauttanen Arctic Resort, Finnish Lapland: Located at Kiilopääntie 9 in Saariselkä, this iconic resort is famous for its glass igloos that allow guests to sleep under the stars and, if lucky, the Northern Lights. In addition to igloos, the resort offers log cabins and kelo-glass hybrids. Pricing for a glass igloo starts at 800 EUR ($850) per night, depending on the season. Booking is best done through their website or by calling +358 16 667 100. Activities include dog sledding, snowmobiling, and visits to Santa's Home, making it ideal for winter enthusiasts. Guests adore the magical Arctic setting and unique accommodation options. However, limited privacy in the igloos and the lack of included meals in some packages are common criticisms.

Fjord Lodges at Manshausen Island, Norway: Situated off the Helgeland Coast, Manshausen Island offers stunning overwater lodges with panoramic views of the sea and surrounding mountains. Designed by architect Snorre Stinessen, these minimalist cabins blend seamlessly with their natural surroundings. Prices start at 4,000 NOK ($380) per night, and bookings can be made online or by contacting +47 75 77 21 44. Accessible via a short ferry ride from Nordskot, this secluded retreat is perfect for kayaking, fishing, or simply soaking in the beauty of the Arctic Circle. Guests love the exclusivity, modern design, and proximity to nature. The drawbacks include the need for advance planning to reach the remote location and limited dining options on-site.

Mid-Range Hotels and Boutique Stays

Wakeup Copenhagen, Borgergade, Copenhagen: Located at Borgergade 9, Wakeup Copenhagen is a budget-friendly hotel that feels anything but cheap. Just a short walk from Nyhavn and the Kongens Nytorv metro station, it offers sleek, modern rooms designed to maximize space and comfort. Rooms start at 600 DKK ($90) per night, making it one of the best-value options in the city center. Booking is easy through their website or by calling +45 44 80 00 00. Guests love its prime location and efficient design, while the lack of in-room coffee makers and minimal storage space are minor drawbacks. It's perfect for those who prioritize location over frills.

Hotel Hellsten, Stockholm: Nestled in the vibrant Vasastan district at Luntmakargatan 68, Hotel Hellsten is a boutique hotel with a touch of personality. Each room is uniquely decorated, blending antique furniture with modern amenities. A highlight is the cozy jazz bar, where live performances create a warm, welcoming atmosphere. Rooms start at 1,400 SEK ($130) per night, and reservations can be made by calling +46 8 661 86 00 or online. The hotel is within walking distance of the Stockholm metro, making it easy to explore the city. Guests appreciate the eclectic decor and friendly staff, though some mention that rooms on the lower floors can be slightly noisy.

Citybox Oslo: For travelers seeking convenience and affordability, Citybox Oslo at Prinsens gate 6 is an excellent choice. This no-frills, self-service hotel offers bright, minimalist rooms at prices starting around 900 NOK ($85) per night. It's just a five-minute walk from Oslo Central Station, making it ideal for travelers arriving by train. Booking can be done online or by contacting +47 21 42 04 80. The hotel's self-check-in kiosks make arrival seamless, and guests often praise the clean, functional rooms. However, the lack of in-room phones and limited on-site dining options might be drawbacks for those seeking more amenities.

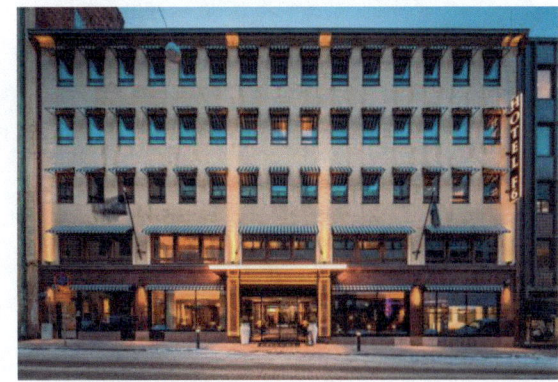

Hotel F6, Helsinki: Situated at Fabianinkatu 6 in Helsinki's city center, Hotel F6 is a family-owned boutique hotel that exudes warmth and elegance. Each room features Nordic-inspired design, with wooden accents and plush bedding. The hotel's courtyard garden and organic breakfast buffet are standout features that guests adore. Rooms start at 190 EUR ($200) per night, and bookings can be made by calling +358 9 6899 660 or via their website. Located just steps from Esplanadi Park and the Design District, it's perfect for exploring Helsinki's vibrant culture. While the hotel's boutique size ensures a personal touch, it also means availability can be limited, so booking early is advised.

Reykjavik Marina – Berjaya Iceland Hotels, Reykjavik: Found at Mýrargata 2 by Reykjavik's old harbor, this quirky boutique hotel combines industrial design with Icelandic charm. Rooms are compact but full of character, and the on-site bar, Slippbarinn, is a popular spot for locals and tourists alike. Rates start at 25,000 ISK ($180) per night, with reservations available online or by calling +354 444 4000. Its location makes it ideal for whale-watching tours and exploring Reykjavik's artistic Grandi district. Guests often highlight the lively atmosphere and unique decor as major perks, though some mention that the bustling bar can make the lobby noisy in the evenings.

Hostels and Budget Lodging

Danhostel Copenhagen City, Copenhagen: Located at H.C. Andersens Boulevard 50, Danhostel Copenhagen City is a five-star hostel that's as stylish as it is affordable. With modern interiors, a lively bar, and panoramic views of the city, it feels more like a boutique hotel than a traditional hostel. A bed in a shared dorm starts at 250 DKK ($35), while private rooms begin at 700 DKK ($100). Booking is simple through their website or by calling +45 33 11 85 85. Just a short walk from Tivoli Gardens and the City Hall Square, it's perfectly positioned for exploring the city. Guests love the clean facilities and social vibe, though the busy atmosphere might not suit those seeking total tranquility.

Generator Stockholm, Stockholm: Found at Torsgatan 10, Generator Stockholm offers a trendy, social experience in the heart of the city. This design-forward hostel features stylish dorms and private rooms, as well as a bar and lounge perfect for meeting fellow travelers.

Prices start at 300 SEK ($30) for a dorm bed and 800 SEK ($80) for private rooms. Reservations can be made online or by calling +46 8 505 292 00. The hostel's location near the central train station makes it ideal for exploring Stockholm's attractions like Gamla Stan and the Vasa Museum. Guests praise its vibrant atmosphere and comfortable beds, though the bar can get noisy in the evenings.

Oslo Hostel Central, Oslo: At Kongens gate 7, Oslo Hostel Central offers a clean, modern, and centrally located budget option. Dorm beds start at 350 NOK ($33), and private rooms are available for around 950 NOK ($90). Booking is available through their website or by contacting +47 23 10 08 00. The hostel includes a free breakfast buffet, a rare perk that adds great value. Its proximity to attractions like the Oslo Opera House and the Aker Brygge waterfront makes it a top choice for travelers. Guests love the welcoming staff and cozy common areas, though the shared bathrooms can feel crowded during peak times.

KEX Hostel, Reykjavik: Located at Skúlagata 28, KEX Hostel combines Icelandic charm with a laid-back, social atmosphere. Set in a repurposed biscuit factory, the hostel features vintage decor, a lively bar, and even a barber shop. Dorm beds start at 7,000 ISK ($50), while private rooms begin at 20,000 ISK ($145). Reservations can be made by calling +354 561 6060 or via their website. KEX's location near Reykjavik's harbor and main shopping street makes it convenient for exploring the city. Guests love the unique character and friendly vibe, though the bar's popularity can sometimes make the common areas crowded.

Hamina Cabin Rentals, Finnish Lakeland: For a more rustic experience, cabin rentals in Finnish Lakeland offer a peaceful escape into nature. Hamina, a small town surrounded by forests and lakes, has a variety of cabins for rent through sites like Lomarengas. Prices start at around 100 EUR ($105) per night, depending on the season and amenities. Most cabins come equipped with saunas, fireplaces, and lake access, making them ideal for relaxation. Guests enjoy fishing, swimming, and hiking in the pristine surroundings. While cabins provide serenity, their remote locations can make transportation a challenge without a car.

Vacation Rentals and Airbnb

Vacation rentals and Airbnb options in Scandinavia provide a unique way to experience the region, often offering more space, privacy, and local charm than traditional hotels. For travelers who prefer the comforts of home, rentals can also be a cost-effective option, especially for families or groups. From stylish apartments in city centers to cozy countryside cottages, these options bring you closer to Scandinavian living while allowing flexibility and value.

Nyhavn Apartment, Copenhagen: Located in the heart of the iconic Nyhavn district, this two-bedroom apartment offers sweeping canal views and a stylish Scandinavian interior. It's perfect for soaking in the vibrant atmosphere of Copenhagen, with top attractions like Tivoli Gardens and Christiansborg Palace just a short walk away. Rates start at 2,500 DKK ($350) per night, making it a great option for families or small groups. Booking is available through Airbnb or by contacting the host directly. Guests rave about the spacious living area and fully equipped kitchen, though the central location can mean some street noise at night.

Gamla Stan Studio, Stockholm: Tucked away in the historic Old Town, this charming studio offers an authentic Swedish experience. The cobblestone streets of Gamla Stan are right outside your door, with landmarks like the Royal Palace and Nobel Museum within minutes. The studio features a modern kitchenette, comfortable furnishings, and enough space for two people. Prices start at 1,400 SEK ($130) per night, significantly less than nearby hotels. Reservations can be made through Airbnb. Guests love the unbeatable location and cozy atmosphere, though the small size might feel limiting for longer stays.

Lofoten Waterfront Cabin, Norway: For a more remote and scenic escape, this waterfront cabin in the Lofoten Islands is hard to beat. Perched right by the sea, it offers stunning views of the dramatic peaks and serene waters that define the region. The cabin accommodates up to four people and includes a kitchenette, outdoor deck, and easy access to hiking and kayaking. Prices start at 3,000 NOK ($285) per night, and bookings are available through Airbnb or directly with local rental agencies. Guests highlight the peaceful surroundings and breathtaking views as major advantages, though the isolated location requires a car to explore the area fully.

Design Loft in Helsinki, Finland: Located in the trendy Kallio district, this modern loft combines industrial design with Finnish minimalism. With an open floor plan, high ceilings, and a private balcony, it's ideal for travelers seeking a stylish urban retreat. Kallio is known for its vibrant nightlife and hip cafes, making it a great base for exploring Helsinki. The loft sleeps up to three people, with rates starting at 180 EUR ($190) per night. Bookings can be made on Airbnb or through the property's website. Guests love the sleek design and lively neighborhood, though street parking can be tricky if you're driving.

Reykjavik Family Home, Iceland: Perfect for families, this three-bedroom home in Reykjavik's quiet Vesturbær neighborhood offers space and comfort just a short walk from the city center. The house features a fully equipped kitchen, spacious living room, and private garden. Nearby, you'll find local swimming pools and the Grandi harbor district, known for its art galleries and eateries. Prices start at 35,000 ISK ($250) per night, providing excellent value compared to hotels in Reykjavik. Reservations are available on Airbnb or by contacting the host directly. Guests appreciate the family-friendly layout and peaceful surroundings, though the residential location means fewer dining options within immediate walking distance.

When comparing costs between hotels and vacation rentals, rentals often provide better value, especially for longer stays or larger groups. For instance, a hotel room in central Copenhagen might cost 2,000 DKK ($280) per night for two people, whereas a two-bedroom apartment like the Nyhavn rental accommodates up to four people for a similar price. Additionally, rentals with kitchens allow you to save on dining out, which can be pricey in Scandinavia.

Choosing the right area for your rental is essential to making the most of your trip. In Copenhagen, Nyhavn and Vesterbro are ideal for their central locations and vibrant atmospheres. Stockholm's Gamla Stan offers charm and history, while Södermalm provides a trendy, artsy vibe. For a serene retreat, Norway's fjord regions or Finland's Lakeland are excellent choices, while Reykjavik's downtown and Vesturbær neighborhoods balance convenience and tranquility.

DINING AND CUISINE

Traditional Scandinavian Dishes

Danish Smørrebrød: These open-faced sandwiches are a staple in Denmark and a feast for both the eyes and the palate. Built on a base of dense rye bread, smørrebrød are topped with a variety of ingredients like pickled herring, roast beef, shrimp, or eggs. One of the most traditional varieties is the herring smørrebrød, garnished with onions, capers, and dill. You'll find smørrebrød in restaurants across Denmark, but locals swear by places like Aamanns Deli in Copenhagen, where prices range from 85 to 120 DKK ($12–$17) per piece. The artistry in their presentation is almost as delightful as their flavor. The only challenge is choosing which topping to try first!

Swedish Meatballs (Köttbullar): Sweden's most famous culinary export, köttbullar, is a dish that warms your heart as much as your stomach. Traditionally made with a mix of beef and pork, these meatballs are seasoned with nutmeg and allspice, pan-fried to golden perfection, and served with creamy gravy, lingonberry jam, and buttery mashed potatoes. While you can find meatballs everywhere from IKEA to fine dining establishments, Oaxen Slip in Stockholm elevates this classic with locally sourced ingredients, priced at about 200 SEK ($18). The combination of sweet and savory flavors is quintessentially Swedish, and every bite takes you deeper into the country's culinary heritage.

Norwegian Salmon: Norway is synonymous with salmon, and once you've tasted it here, you'll understand why. Whether smoked, grilled, or cured as gravlaks, Norwegian salmon is celebrated for its rich flavor and silky texture. The dish often comes served with dill, mustard sauce, and boiled potatoes or rye bread. For an unforgettable experience, try it at Fjord Restaurant in Oslo, where dishes featuring salmon start at 250 NOK ($24). The quality of Norwegian salmon is second to none, largely thanks to the country's pristine waters. Eating it fresh in Norway feels like a privilege, a taste of the sea's purest offering.

Finnish Reindeer Dishes: In Finnish Lapland, reindeer meat is not just a delicacy—it's a part of daily life and cultural identity. Sautéed **reindeer**, or **poronkäristys**, is one of the most traditional ways to enjoy it. Thinly sliced meat is cooked with butter, onions, and a touch of salt, then served with mashed potatoes and lingonberries. The dish is hearty, warming, and deeply satisfying. One of the best places to try it is at Restaurant Nili in Rovaniemi, where prices start at 30 EUR ($32). The reindeer's lean, gamey flavor makes it a must-try for adventurous eaters, though it's also surprisingly approachable for those new to wild meats.

Icelandic Skyr: While technically a cheese, skyr is often enjoyed like yogurt and has been a part of Icelandic cuisine for over 1,000 years. Creamy, tangy, and packed with protein, it's a favorite for breakfast, dessert, or a snack. Skyr is traditionally served with fresh berries, a drizzle of honey, or a sprinkle of granola. You can find it in supermarkets and cafes across Iceland, but for a more authentic experience, head to Skyrgerðin in Hveragerði, where they make it the old-fashioned way. A bowl costs about 1,200 ISK ($9). Light yet filling, skyr embodies the Icelandic philosophy of making the most of simple, wholesome ingredients.

Street Food and Local Markets

Torvehallerne, Copenhagen: In the heart of Denmark's capital, Torvehallerne is a foodie paradise that combines a modern aesthetic with traditional Danish flavors. Located at Frederiksborggade 21, this market features over 60 stalls offering everything from artisanal chocolates to freshly baked pastries. Smørrebrød, the iconic Danish open-faced sandwich, is a highlight here, and Hallernes Smørrebrød serves some of the best in the city for around 75 DKK ($11) each. For seafood lovers, fresh oysters at Hav are a must-try. Easily accessible by metro at Nørreport Station, Torvehallerne offers a vibrant, welcoming atmosphere. While it's slightly pricier than other markets, the variety and quality make it well worth a visit.

Östermalm Food Hall, Stockholm: A visit to Stockholm wouldn't be complete without exploring the iconic Östermalm Food Hall at Östermalmstorg 31. This historic market, which dates back to the 1880s, was recently renovated to blend its old-world charm with modern touches. Here, you'll find everything from Swedish meatballs and gravlax to gourmet cheeses and freshly baked bread. Lisa Elmqvist, a family-run seafood vendor, is particularly beloved for its classic fish dishes, with prices starting at 150 SEK ($14). The market's central location and cozy ambiance make it an easy stop for lunch or a quick bite while exploring Stockholm. Some might find it a bit touristy, but its enduring reputation ensures it remains a favorite among locals and visitors alike.

Fisketorget, Bergen: Nestled on the harborfront, Fisketorget (Fish Market) in Bergen is a feast for the senses. This outdoor and indoor market offers an array of fresh seafood, from salmon and shrimp to the adventurous option of whale meat. You can enjoy a piping hot bowl of fish soup for around 100 NOK ($10) or indulge in a seafood platter at Fjellskål, where prices range from 300 to 500 NOK ($28–$47). The market's vibrant atmosphere and unbeatable waterfront views make it an unforgettable experience. It's conveniently located near Bryggen Wharf, a UNESCO World Heritage Site. While the outdoor stalls are seasonal, the indoor market operates year-round, making it a must-visit no matter when you're in Bergen.

Helsinki Old Market Hall, Helsinki: A stone's throw from the city's harbor at Eteläranta, Helsinki Old Market Hall has been serving customers since 1889. This historic venue offers a warm, inviting space to sample Finnish specialties like salmon soup, reindeer jerky, and Karelian pasties. A bowl of creamy salmon soup at Story restaurant, for instance, costs around 12 EUR ($13), making it an affordable yet delicious meal. The market is easily accessible from Helsinki's city center, either on foot or by tram. Visitors love the friendly vendors and authentic flavors, though the limited seating can be a challenge during peak hours.

Reykjavik Street Food Stalls, Reykjavik: While Iceland doesn't have the sprawling markets of its Scandinavian neighbors, its street food scene is vibrant and growing. Around the Reykjavik harbor and main streets like Laugavegur, you'll find stalls serving traditional lamb soup, hot dogs, and fresh fish. Bæjarins Beztu Pylsur, Iceland's most famous hot dog stand, offers a legendary hot dog for around 600 ISK ($4). The charm of Reykjavik's street food lies in its simplicity and quality, though some might find the options less diverse compared to larger markets.

Fine Dining and Michelin-Star Restaurants

Noma, Copenhagen: Noma is not just a restaurant; it's a culinary phenomenon. Located at Refshalevej 96, this three-Michelin-starred establishment is led by Chef René Redzepi, who has revolutionized Nordic cuisine. The menu changes with the seasons, offering three distinct experiences: the Ocean menu in winter, the Vegetable menu in summer, and the Game and Forest menu in autumn. Prices start at 3,900 DKK ($560) for the tasting menu, with wine pairings available for an additional 2,200 DKK ($320). Reservations are notoriously difficult to secure and open three times a year on their website. Guests are often awestruck by the creativity and attention to detail in every dish. The only downside? The price and waitlist might require some planning, but the experience is worth every effort.

Frantzén, Stockholm: Located at Klara Norra kyrkogata 26, Frantzén is Stockholm's pride and joy, boasting three Michelin stars and a reputation for culinary artistry. Chef Björn Frantzén combines Swedish traditions with Japanese and French influences, resulting in a menu that's as adventurous as it is refined. The full tasting menu costs 5,000 SEK ($460), with optional wine pairings starting at 2,000 SEK ($185). Booking can be done online or by calling +46 8 20 85 80. The restaurant offers an intimate atmosphere with just 23 seats, ensuring a personalized experience. Guests rave about the seamless progression of flavors and the impeccable service, though the exclusivity means reservations can be hard to come by.

Maaemo, Oslo: Perched at Dronning Eufemias gate 23, Maaemo is a three-star Michelin restaurant that celebrates Norway's natural bounty. Chef Esben Holmboe Bang crafts an immersive tasting menu that highlights ingredients like Arctic char, wild herbs, and reindeer. The dining experience costs 4,200 NOK ($390) per person, with wine pairings adding another 2,800 NOK ($260). Reservations can be made on their website or by calling +47 91 99 48 05. The minimalist, Nordic-inspired setting perfectly complements the food, creating a harmonious experience. While the price is steep, guests consistently describe it as a once-in-a-lifetime meal that's both innovative and deeply rooted in Norwegian heritage.

KOKS, Faroe Islands: For a truly unique adventure, KOKS in the Faroe Islands is an unmissable experience. Located at Leynar, this two-Michelin-starred restaurant offers a tasting menu centered around local, sustainable ingredients like fermented lamb, seaweed, and wild herbs. The menu costs 2,500 DKK ($360), with optional beverage pairings starting at 1,500 DKK ($215). Reservations can be made via their website or by contacting +298 33 80 60. Guests are shuttled to the restaurant's remote location, adding to the sense of exclusivity and adventure. While the flavors are bold and sometimes challenging, diners leave with a profound appreciation for Faroese culture and cuisine.

Dill, Reykjavik: Iceland's first and only Michelin-starred restaurant, Dill, is located at Laugavegur 59 in Reykjavik. Chef Gunnar Karl Gíslason showcases Icelandic ingredients in a seven-course tasting menu that costs around 21,000 ISK ($150), with wine pairings for an additional 12,000 ISK ($85). The intimate setting and focus on sustainability make every dish feel like a love letter to Iceland's rugged beauty. Reservations can be made online or by calling +354 552 1522. Guests adore the thoughtful presentations and surprising flavors, though some note that the minimalist portions might leave hearty appetites wanting more.

Coffee Culture and Local Drinks

Swedish Fika: In Sweden, coffee is more than a drink—it's a ritual known as *fika*, a daily pause to enjoy coffee and something sweet with friends or colleagues. It's a time to relax and catch up, embodying the Swedish ethos of work-life balance. Traditionally paired with cinnamon buns (*kanelbullar*) or cardamom twists (*kardemummabullar*), fika feels like a warm hug for your soul. Coffeehouses like Vete-Katten in Stockholm are quintessential spots to experience this tradition, with a cup of coffee costing around 40 SEK ($4). Fika is about slowing down in a fast-paced world, but be warned—it's easy to get addicted to the comforting rhythm of this daily indulgence.

Aquavit: If you're looking for a drink that embodies the spirit of Scandinavia, Aquavit (or

Akvavit) is it. This distilled spirit, flavored with caraway or dill, is a staple at festive occasions across Denmark, Norway, and Sweden. It's often served chilled in small glasses and paired with hearty foods like herring or smoked salmon. One of the most famous brands, Aalborg Aquavit from Denmark, can be found in most liquor stores, with a 700ml bottle priced around 300 DKK ($45). While its strong, herbal flavor might take some getting used to, it's an essential part of Scandinavian celebrations, from midsummer to Christmas. The downside? It can pack a punch, so pace yourself if you're new to it.

Nordic Craft Beers: Scandinavia's craft beer scene has exploded in recent years, with microbreweries producing some of the most innovative and flavorful beers in the world. Denmark's Mikkeller, Stockholm's Nya Carnegiebryggeriet, and Norway's Lervig are just a few names making waves internationally. At Øl & Brød in Copenhagen, you can enjoy Mikkeller's beers paired with classic Danish smørrebrød, with a pint averaging 75 DKK ($11). The diversity of flavors, from hoppy IPAs to rich stouts, ensures there's something for every beer lover. The downside? Alcohol prices in Scandinavia can be steep, but the quality makes it worth the splurge.

Icelandic Brennivín: Known as the "Black Death" for its bold flavor, Brennivín is Iceland's signature spirit. Made from fermented potatoes and flavored with caraway seeds, it's traditionally served alongside fermented shark (*hákarl*)—a pairing not for the faint-hearted. A 500ml bottle of Brennivín costs about 5,000 ISK ($36) at the state-run Vínbúðin stores. While the taste can be polarizing, its cultural significance is undeniable, and it's a must-try for adventurous drinkers. Just don't let its nickname scare you—it's smoother than it sounds, especially when enjoyed responsibly.

Cloudberry Liquor: Scandinavia's wilderness is home to unique berries, and cloudberries are among the most prized. These golden-orange berries are used to create a sweet, tangy liquor that's often enjoyed as a dessert drink or poured over ice cream. Brands like Lapponia Cloudberry Liqueur from Finland make it easy to bring this Nordic treat home, with bottles priced at around 200 SEK ($18). Its delicate flavor captures the essence of the Nordic forests, making it a perfect way to toast your Scandinavian adventure. The only downside? It can be hard to find outside the region, so stock up while you're there.

Vegetarian and Vegan Dining

Plant Power Food, Copenhagen: Located at Fælledvej 15 in Nørrebro, Plant Power Food is a standout in Denmark's plant-based scene. Their menu focuses on seasonal ingredients, with dishes like beet tartare and mushroom risotto showcasing bold flavors and artistic presentation. Prices are reasonable for the quality, with main courses starting at 135 DKK ($20). Easily accessible by metro, this cozy spot is perfect for a casual dinner or celebrating a special occasion. Guests rave about the warm atmosphere and inventive dishes, though the small space means reservations are a good idea.

Hermans, Stockholm: Set on the picturesque Södermalm island at Fjällgatan 23B, Hermans offers not only delicious vegan food but also breathtaking views of Stockholm's harbor. Their buffet-style dining features an ever-changing menu of global-inspired dishes, from Moroccan stews to fresh salads, all made with organic ingredients. Prices are around 225 SEK ($21) for the buffet, making it great value for those with a big appetite. Booking is available online or by calling +46 8 643 94 80. While the food and views are excellent, the busy atmosphere during peak times might not suit those seeking a quieter dining experience.

Kaf, Oslo: A trendy café located at Schweigaards gate 56, Kaf is a vegan hotspot that's perfect for everything from breakfast to dinner. Their menu includes colorful smoothie bowls, hearty sandwiches, and indulgent desserts like raw chocolate cake. Prices start at 90 NOK ($9) for light dishes, with more substantial options around 180 NOK ($17). Easily reachable by public transport, Kaf is a favorite among locals for its cozy vibe and high-quality ingredients. While the menu is smaller than some other places, the flavors and presentation more than make up for it.

Yes Yes Yes, Helsinki: Found at Iso Roobertinkatu 1, Yes Yes Yes is a vibrant vegetarian restaurant that feels like a celebration of food and life. Their menu is packed with creative dishes, such as halloumi fries with pomegranate and house-made hummus served with warm flatbread. Prices for small plates start at 8 EUR ($8.50), while mains range around 20 EUR ($21). The colorful interiors and lively atmosphere make it a fun spot for dinner with friends or a casual date. Guests often highlight the friendly service and inventive flavors, though the popularity of the restaurant can make it noisy at times.

Kaffi Vínyl, Reykjavik: At Hverfisgata 76, Kaffi Vínyl is Reykjavik's go-to vegan café, combining delicious plant-based meals with a love for vinyl records. Their vegan burgers and creamy cashew-based pasta dishes are crowd favorites, with prices averaging 2,500 ISK ($18). The relaxed atmosphere and curated music collection add a unique charm, making it a must-visit for food and music lovers alike. While the space is cozy and welcoming, it can fill up quickly, especially during lunch hours.

THINGS TO DO AND OUTDOOR ACTIVITIES

Winter Adventures

Dog sledding is one of the most iconic winter activities, giving you a chance to feel the exhilaration of gliding across frozen landscapes powered by a team of eager huskies. In Finnish Lapland, the snowy trails near Rovaniemi are perfect for this adventure. Guided tours, such as those offered by Bearhill Husky, take you through silent forests and across open tundras, with prices starting around €150 for a half-day experience. You'll learn how to harness the dogs and steer the sled before heading out into the wilderness, the only sounds being the swish of the sled and the panting of the huskies. The experience is accessible for all, and getting there is simple, with regular flights to Rovaniemi and transfers to the nearby kennels. Dog sledding is not just a thrill; it's a way to connect with the natural beauty and traditions of the Arctic.

Reindeer safaris are another quintessential experience, offering a quieter, more traditional glimpse into Lapland's culture. Reindeer herding has been a cornerstone of Sami life for centuries, and today, visitors can join herders for a journey through snowy forests. Places like Tromsø in Norway or Kiruna in Sweden are ideal for these safaris. At Sami camps like Tromsø Arctic Reindeer, you'll meet the herders, feed the reindeer, and even enjoy a sleigh ride under the stars. Prices typically start at NOK 1,500 ($140), and many tours include a warm meal in a traditional Sami tent, complete with stories about their way of life. The serenity of gliding through the snow behind these gentle creatures is unforgettable, and the cultural insights make it even more special.

For those who enjoy tranquil moments in nature, ice fishing offers a peaceful yet exciting way to embrace the Nordic winter. Imagine sitting on a frozen lake, bundled in warm layers, as you wait for a nibble on your line. In Finnish Lakeland or northern Norway, guided ice fishing tours provide all the equipment and expertise needed, with prices starting around €80 for a few hours. At Lake Inari in Finland, you might even catch trout or Arctic char. Many tours combine ice fishing with a cozy break by a campfire, complete with hot drinks and snacks. Getting to these locations often involves a scenic drive or snowmobile ride, adding to the adventure.

Of course, no winter trip to Scandinavia is complete without chasing the **Northern Lights.** The aurora borealis is one of nature's most spectacular displays, and the Arctic regions of Norway, Sweden, and Finland are among the best places to witness it. Tromsø, Norway, is often called the "Gateway to the Arctic" and is a hub for Northern Lights tours. Companies like Chasing Lights offer guided trips for around NOK 1,800 ($170), taking you to remote locations with the best viewing conditions. In Swedish Lapland, the Aurora Sky Station in Abisko National Park is renowned for its clear skies, while Finnish resorts like Kakslauttanen provide glass igloos for viewing the lights from the warmth of your bed. The best time to visit is between November and March, with darker, cloudless nights offering the best chances.

For adrenaline junkies, *ice climbing* provides a thrilling way to explore Scandinavia's frozen landscapes. In Rjukan, Norway, one of Europe's premier ice climbing destinations, sheer walls of frozen waterfalls await. Guided tours, such as those offered by Rjukan Ice Climbers, cater to all skill levels and cost around NOK 2,000 ($185) for a day. Professional guides ensure safety as you strap on crampons, grab your ice axe, and ascend the glistening walls. The combination of physical challenge and breathtaking views makes this an unforgettable experience, though it's best suited for those with a moderate level of fitness.

Summer Outdoor Activities

Hiking in Norway is like stepping into a painting, where every turn reveals a view more stunning than the last. The country's fjords, mountains, and glaciers offer trails for every skill level, but one of the most iconic hikes is to Pulpit Rock (*Preikestolen*). Located near Stavanger, this four-hour round-trip hike leads you to a flat-topped cliff that soars 604 meters above Lysefjord. The panoramic views from the top are breathtaking, making it a must-do for outdoor enthusiasts. Getting there is straightforward, with ferries and buses running regularly from Stavanger to the trailhead. Guided tours are available for around 700 NOK ($65) per person, including transportation. For seasoned hikers seeking more of a challenge, Trolltunga near Odda offers a demanding but rewarding adventure. The 10- to 12-hour trek covers 28 kilometers, culminating in a stunning view from a cliff that juts out like a tongue over Lake Ringedalsvatnet. Summer, from June to September, is the ideal time to explore these trails, as the weather is mild and the days are long.

Kayaking in Sweden is a serene and immersive way to experience the country's natural beauty, especially in the **Stockholm Archipelago**. With over 30,000 islands scattered across the Baltic Sea, the archipelago is a paradise for paddlers. Kayak rentals and guided tours are readily available in Stockholm, with prices starting at 600 SEK ($55) for a half-day rental. Companies like Green Trails offer guided kayaking adventures that include equipment, instruction, and even picnics on secluded islands. As you paddle through calm waters, you'll pass rocky shores, colorful cottages, and maybe even spot seals basking in the sun. For a more remote experience, the Bohuslän Coast in western Sweden offers stunning granite cliffs and clear waters. The best time to kayak is during the summer months, when the weather is warm, and the sea is calm.

In Finland, the **Midnight Sun i**s one of nature's most magical phenomena, offering nearly 24 hours of daylight in the summer months. This unique experience is best enjoyed in the northern regions of Finnish Lapland, where the sun doesn't set for weeks. One of the best ways to embrace this endless daylight is through evening hikes or midnight canoe trips on serene lakes. Towns like Rovaniemi and Inari serve as great bases, with local guides offering excursions that showcase the surreal beauty of the Midnight Sun. For around €100, you can join a guided canoe tour, gliding silently across the water as the sun hovers just above the horizon, painting the sky in shades of gold and pink. The Midnight Sun season runs from mid-May to late July, and its ethereal glow creates a sense of timelessness, making every moment feel extraordinary.

Horseback riding in Iceland is another must-try adventure that lets you experience the country's landscapes in a truly unique way. The Icelandic horse, known for its sturdy build and smooth gait, is a symbol of the country's heritage. Riding tours are available across Iceland, but the lava fields near Reykjavik or the black sand beaches of Vik are particularly popular. Companies like Ishestar offer guided rides starting at 11,000 ISK ($75) for a two-hour trek. These tours take you through dramatic scenery, from volcanic landscapes to lush valleys, all while riding a horse whose gentle temperament makes it suitable for beginners and experienced riders alike. Getting to Reykjavik is easy, with regular flights from major cities, and most stables are within an hour's drive of the capital. Summer, from June to August, is the best time for horseback riding, as the mild weather and vibrant landscapes add to the experience.

Wildlife and Nature Excursions

Whale watching in Norway is an adventure that brings you up close to the giants of the sea. The northern town of Tromsø, often referred to as the "Gateway to the Arctic," is one of the best places to embark on this thrilling excursion. From November to January, the fjords around Tromsø become a feeding ground for humpback whales and orcas as they follow the migrating herring. Guided tours depart from Tromsø Harbor, with companies like Arctic Adventure Tours offering trips starting at 1,200 NOK ($110). These tours take you out on RIB (rigid inflatable boats) or larger vessels, ensuring both safety and excellent views.

The sight of a humpback whale breaching against a backdrop of snow-covered mountains is nothing short of magical. Tromsø is well-connected by flights from Oslo and other Scandinavian cities, making it an accessible gateway to this Arctic experience. While winter is prime whale-watching season, summer also offers opportunities in southern Norway, where sperm whales and minke whales are often spotted near the Lofoten Islands.

Puffin spotting in Iceland is a charming experience that feels straight out of a nature documentary. These colorful seabirds, with their vibrant orange beaks and playful demeanor, are a joy to watch. The Westman Islands (Vestmannaeyjar), just off Iceland's southern coast, are home to one of the largest puffin colonies in the world. From May to August, millions of puffins nest here, and boat tours like those offered by Ribsafari take you close to their rocky cliffside habitats. Prices start at 10,000 ISK ($70) for a one-hour tour. Getting to the Westman Islands involves a ferry ride from Landeyjahöfn, about a two-hour drive from Reykjavik. Alternatively, you can spot puffins closer to the capital at Lundey, or "Puffin Island," where tours depart from Reykjavik's Old Harbor for around 5,500 ISK ($40). The best time to visit is early morning or late evening when the birds are most active, and their comical waddles and social interactions are sure to bring a smile to your face.

For those drawn to the mystery of the *forest, bear-watching in Finland* offers a thrilling yet tranquil way to connect with nature. In the dense woodlands of Finnish Karelia, near the Russian border, brown bears roam freely in their natural habitat. Guided bear-watching tours provide a safe and respectful way to observe these magnificent creatures. Martinselkonen Wilds Centre, located near Suomussalmi, is a renowned destination for these excursions. From May to September, you can spend an evening or even an overnight stay in a secluded hide, watching bears emerge from the forest in search of food. Prices for a half-day bear-watching experience start at €150, including a knowledgeable guide and use of a comfortable hide equipped with large viewing windows. The center is accessible by car from Kajaani Airport, with transfers available upon request. While bears are the main attraction, the forest is also home to wolverines, lynxes, and a variety of bird species, adding to the richness of the experience.

Scandinavia's wildlife adventures are best enjoyed during the specific seasons when these animals are most active. Whale watching peaks during the winter months in Norway, while puffin spotting and bear-watching are summer activities. Each excursion offers not only a chance to see incredible animals but also an opportunity to immerse yourself in the breathtaking landscapes that define this region. The fjords, cliffs, and forests are as much a part of the experience as the wildlife itself.

ART, CULTURE, AND ENTERTAINMENT

Museums and Art Galleries

The National Gallery in Oslo, Norway, is a treasure trove of Norwegian and international art, and its centerpiece is one of the most famous paintings in the world: The Scream by Edvard Munch. Located at Universitetsgata 13, this gallery is part of the National Museum of Norway and recently moved to a stunning new facility on Oslo's waterfront. Here, you'll find not only Munch's masterpieces but also works by other Norwegian greats like J.C. Dahl and Harriet Backer, alongside international artists like Monet and Picasso. Tickets cost 180 NOK ($17) and can be purchased online or at the museum. Getting there is easy, with the Oslo Central Station just a short walk away. Visitors rave about the thoughtfully curated exhibits and the expansive, light-filled galleries that offer a serene viewing experience. The best time to visit is in the morning, when the crowds are lighter, allowing you to fully immerse yourself in the art.

In Denmark, the **Louisiana Museum of Modern Art** is an absolute must-visit for art lovers. Situated in Humlebæk, about 35 kilometers north of Copenhagen, the museum is perched on a bluff overlooking the Øresund Strait. Its location alone is breathtaking, but the collection inside is just as impressive. The Louisiana is known for its extensive modern and contemporary art collection, featuring works by artists such as Giacometti, Yayoi Kusama, and Louise Bourgeois. Temporary exhibitions often feature cutting-edge installations that challenge and inspire. Tickets cost 145 DKK ($21) for adults and can be booked online or purchased at the entrance. Getting there involves a 35-minute train ride from Copenhagen Central Station, followed by a 10-minute walk. The museum's sculpture park and outdoor terraces provide a perfect spot to take in the surrounding beauty. Visitors often mention the seamless integration of art, architecture, and nature as a highlight of their trip. Louisiana is best enjoyed on a clear day, allowing you to explore its indoor and outdoor spaces fully.

Finland's Ateneum Art Museum in Helsinki is a beacon of Finnish cultural heritage. Located at Kaivokatu 2, right across from the Helsinki Central Railway Station, the museum is home to the country's most extensive collection of classical art. From the romantic landscapes of Akseli Gallen-Kallela to the evocative portraits of Helene Schjerfbeck, the Ateneum offers a deep dive into Finnish identity and artistry.

Tickets cost 20 EUR ($21), and audio guides are available to enhance your experience. The museum also features rotating exhibitions that bring international art to Finnish audiences, ensuring there's always something new to discover. After exploring the galleries, the museum café is a great place to unwind with a coffee and traditional Finnish pastry. The Ateneum is especially lovely in spring and summer when Helsinki's vibrant streets add to the lively atmosphere around the museum.

For something truly unique, the ***ARoS Aarhus Art Museum*** in Aarhus, Denmark, offers an experience that blends art with architectural wonder. The museum's standout feature is Your Rainbow Panorama, a circular walkway of colored glass atop the building. Created by Olafur Eliasson, this installation provides a 360-degree view of the city through a kaleidoscope of colors. Inside, ARoS houses an impressive collection of Danish Golden Age art, modern works, and provocative contemporary installations. Located at Aros Allé 2, the museum is easily accessible from Aarhus Central Station, just a 10-minute walk away. Tickets cost 160 DKK ($23), and visitors often spend hours exploring the diverse exhibitions. ARoS is particularly captivating in the late afternoon when the sunlight transforms *Your Rainbow Panorama* into a glowing masterpiece.

In Reykjavik, Iceland, the ***National Gallery of Iceland at Fríkirkjuvegur 7*** is a hidden gem that celebrates Icelandic and international art. The museum's permanent collection includes works by prominent Icelandic artists like Jóhannes Sveinsson Kjarval, whose paintings capture the island's rugged landscapes with a sense of mysticism. Admission costs 2,000 ISK ($15), and the museum's central location makes it a convenient stop while exploring the city. For a more contemporary vibe, head to the Reykjavik Art Museum, which spans three locations and showcases everything from cutting-edge installations to thematic retrospectives. The best time to visit Reykjavik's art scene is during the summer months when extended daylight hours provide extra time for exploration.

Music and Festivals

Roskilde Festival in Denmark is legendary, and for good reason. Held every summer in the town of Roskilde, about 35 kilometers west of Copenhagen, this festival draws music lovers from around the globe. It's one of Europe's largest and oldest music festivals, dating back to 1971. The festival spans eight days and features a mix of international superstars and emerging artists across genres, from rock and hip-hop to electronic and world music. Recent lineups have included artists like Taylor Swift, Kendrick Lamar, and The Strokes. Tickets for the full festival cost around 2,400 DKK ($340), with one-day passes available for approximately 1,200 DKK ($170). Camping is a big part of the Roskilde experience, and the festival grounds transform into a vibrant community of music fans. To get there, take a 30-minute train ride from Copenhagen to Roskilde Station, followed by a short walk or shuttle to the venue. The festival typically takes place in late June or early July, and the long summer days make it an unforgettable experience.

In Sweden, the Stockholm Jazz Festival is a celebration of smooth rhythms and soulful melodies that captivates audiences every October. This prestigious event has been running since 1980 and showcases a mix of Swedish and international jazz talent. Venues are spread across the city, including iconic locations like the Stockholm Concert Hall and Fasching Jazz Club. Past performers have included legends like Herbie Hancock and contemporary stars like Norah Jones. Tickets vary by venue and performance, with single concert prices starting at around 300 SEK ($28). For those who want to immerse themselves in the festival atmosphere, passes for multiple events are also available. Stockholm is easy to navigate, and many festival venues are within walking distance of the city center or accessible by public transport. The crisp autumn air and cozy venues add to the festival's charm, making it an ideal way to experience the city's cultural scene.

For those who crave something heavier, the Inferno Metal Festival in Oslo, Norway, is a must-attend event. Held every Easter weekend, this festival is a mecca for metalheads, attracting fans and bands from around the world. The event takes place at venues like Rockefeller Music Hall and features a lineup of black metal, death metal, and other extreme genres. Previous headliners have included legends like Emperor, Dimmu Borgir, and Opeth. Tickets for the full festival cost around 2,000 NOK ($185), with single-day passes available for approximately 800 NOK ($75). Oslo's compact city center makes it easy to explore during the day before diving into the festival's electrifying performances at night. Getting to the venues is straightforward, with most located near public transport hubs like Oslo Central Station. The Inferno Metal Festival isn't just a music event—it's a community gathering, with workshops, panels, and meet-and-greets that make it a holistic experience for metal fans.

Literature and Folklore

In Denmark, Hans Christian Andersen's legacy is everywhere. Born in Odense in 1805, this beloved author gave the world some of its most cherished fairy tales, including *The Little Mermaid, The Ugly Duckling, and *The Emperor's New Clothes*. To step into Andersen's world, start with a visit to the Hans Christian Andersen Museum at Bangs Boder 29, Odense. The museum beautifully showcases his life and works through interactive exhibits, manuscripts, and personal artifacts. Admission costs 150 DKK ($22), and it's easily accessible by train from Copenhagen in just 90 minutes. As you wander the cobblestone streets of Odense, it's easy to imagine Andersen drawing inspiration from the charming surroundings of his childhood. The best time to visit is in the spring or summer when the town comes alive with festivals celebrating his stories, complete with theatrical performances and storytelling sessions.

Norse mythology, with its gods, giants, and epic battles, has shaped the cultural identity of Scandinavia for centuries. In Norway, the myths come alive in the Viking Ship Museum at Huk Aveny 35, Oslo. This extraordinary museum houses some of the best-preserved Viking ships in the world, including the Oseberg and Gokstad ships, which date back over 1,000 years. These vessels, once used for both exploration and burial rites, offer a tangible link to the tales of gods like Thor, Odin, and Loki. Tickets cost 120 NOK ($11), and the museum is a short bus ride from Oslo Central Station. For a deeper dive into Norse mythology, head to Bergen, where guided tours explore the landscapes believed to have inspired these ancient stories. Fjords, waterfalls, and mountains all feature prominently in the myths, and seeing them in person adds a layer of wonder to the tales.

Iceland is where Viking legends and sagas truly come to life. Known as the Land of Fire and Ice, Iceland's dramatic landscapes have inspired some of the most compelling stories of heroism and exploration. The Saga Museum in Reykjavik, located at Grandagarður 2, offers an immersive journey into these tales, using life-like figures to bring characters and events to life. Admission costs 2,500 ISK ($18), and the museum is a short walk from the city center. For a more hands-on experience, visit Thingvellir National Park, a UNESCO World Heritage Site where Iceland's early parliament, the Althing, was established in 930 AD. This site, with its dramatic rift valley and crystal-clear waters, feels like stepping into the pages of a saga. Summer, with its long days and mild weather, is the ideal time to explore the park.

Throughout Scandinavia, folklore remains an integral part of daily life, from trolls lurking in Norwegian forests to the mischievous elves of Iceland. In Sweden, the tales of Selma Lagerlöf, the first woman to win the Nobel Prize in Literature, are a testament to the enduring power of folklore. Her novel *The Wonderful Adventures of Nils* captures the magic of Sweden's landscapes and traditions, and a visit to her home in Sunne, Värmland, offers a glimpse into her creative world. The museum, open seasonally, is surrounded by the forests and lakes that inspired her stories. Tickets cost around 120 SEK ($11), and Sunne is easily reachable by train from Stockholm.

7-DAY ITINERARY

Day 1: Copenhagen, Denmark

Morning: Nyhavn and a Canal Tour

Start your day in Nyhavn, Copenhagen's iconic waterfront district. This 17th-century harbor, located at the end of Kongens Nytorv, is a picture-perfect spot where colorful buildings line the canal, and wooden ships bob gently on the water. Originally a bustling port for traders and sailors, Nyhavn is now a lively hub filled with cafes and restaurants. Begin your morning with a leisurely breakfast at one of its charming spots, such as Nyhavns Færgekro, where a traditional Danish breakfast platter costs around 200 DKK ($30). Enjoy freshly baked bread, cheese, smoked salmon, and pastries as you soak in the serene view of the canal.

After breakfast, embark on a canal tour to see the city from the water. Companies like Netto-Bådene offer hour-long tours for 60 DKK ($9), departing from Nyhavn or Gammel Strand. You'll glide past major landmarks like the Opera House, the Little Mermaid statue, and Amalienborg Palace, home to the Danish royal family. The guide provides fascinating insights into Copenhagen's history and architecture, making it an excellent introduction to the city. Morning is the best time for this activity as the light is perfect for photos and the canals are less crowded.

Afternoon: Exploring Christiania and Local Culture

After the canal tour, take a short stroll or bike ride to Freetown Christiania, an alternative community in the Christianshavn district. This self-proclaimed autonomous neighborhood, founded in the 1970s, is a vibrant and eclectic enclave with its own rules and way of life. As you walk through its colorful streets, you'll encounter unique artwork, organic cafes, and local craft shops. Stop by Månefiskeren for a cup of organic coffee or a light lunch, with meals priced around 80 DKK ($12). Be respectful when exploring Christiania, as photography is restricted in certain areas, especially along Pusher Street.

For a deeper dive into local culture, visit the Church of Our Saviour, just a short walk from Christiania. Its famous corkscrew spire offers one of the best views of the city. Climbing to the top costs 65 DKK ($10), and while the narrow stairs can be a bit daunting, the panoramic vista is worth every step. On clear days, you can see all the way to Sweden!

Evening: Tivoli Gardens and Michelin-Starred Dining

As the afternoon fades, head to Tivoli Gardens, located at Vesterbrogade 3, near Copenhagen Central Station. Opened in 1843, this enchanting amusement park is one of the oldest in the world and continues to captivate visitors with its blend of nostalgia and modern attractions. Admission costs 145 DKK ($21), with additional fees for rides. Whether you're enjoying the carousel, strolling through beautifully landscaped gardens, or catching a live performance, Tivoli is magical in the early evening when the park begins to light up.

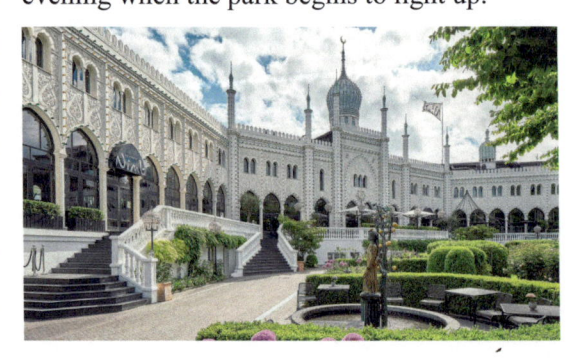

As night falls, end your day with an unforgettable dining experience at one of Copenhagen's Michelin-starred restaurants.

Geranium, located at Per Henrik Lings Allé 4, is a three-star establishment known for its innovative approach to Nordic cuisine. The seasonal tasting menu, crafted by Chef Rasmus Kofoed, costs 3,200 DKK ($475) per person, with wine pairings available for an additional 2,000 DKK ($300). The experience is a symphony of flavors and artistry, featuring dishes like wild duck with forest berries and celeriac baked in hazelnut leaves. Reservations are essential, as Geranium is often booked months in advance.

Alternatively, if you prefer something more casual but equally exquisite, head to Kadeau at Wildersgade 10B. This two-Michelin-starred restaurant highlights the flavors of Denmark's Bornholm Island with a tasting menu priced at 2,500 DKK ($370). The intimate atmosphere and attention to detail make it a perfect finale to your day.

Practical Tips

Copenhagen is a bike-friendly city, and renting a bike for the day costs around 120 DKK ($18). This is a convenient and eco-friendly way to get around, especially if you plan to visit multiple locations. Alternatively, the city's efficient public transport system, including buses and the metro, makes navigating easy. A 24-hour City Pass for unlimited travel within central zones costs 80 DKK ($12).

Summer is the ideal time to visit, as the long daylight hours allow you to maximize your exploration. However, autumn and winter bring their own charm, with cozy cafes and festive decorations enhancing the city's allure.

Day 2: Stockholm, Sweden

Morning: Gamla Stan and the Royal Palace

Start your day in Gamla Stan, Stockholm's Old Town and one of the best-preserved medieval city centers in Europe. Walking its cobblestone streets feels like stepping back in time, with colorful 17th-century buildings, quaint cafes, and charming squares around every corner. Begin your exploration at Stortorget, the main square, where you'll find the Nobel Prize Museum. If you're interested, the museum offers insight into the legacy of the Nobel Prizes, and tickets cost 130 SEK ($12).

Next, head to the Royal Palace, located at Slottsbacken 1, which is still the official residence of the Swedish monarchy. This stunning Baroque building is one of the largest palaces in Europe, with over 600 rooms and several museums. Admission costs 160 SEK ($15) and includes access to the Royal Apartments, the Treasury, and the Gustav III Museum of Antiquities. Don't miss the changing of the guard ceremony, which takes place daily at noon during the summer and a bit earlier in the off-season. The palace is easily accessible from Gamla Stan's metro station, and morning is the best time to visit to avoid crowds.

Afternoon: Vasa Museum and ABBA Museum

After soaking in the history of Gamla Stan, make your way to Djurgården, an island dedicated to Stockholm's cultural attractions. Begin with the Vasa Museum at Galärvarvsvägen 14, home to the only fully intact 17th-century warship ever salvaged. The Vasa sank on its maiden voyage in 1628 and was raised from the seabed over 300 years later. The museum offers a fascinating glimpse into maritime history, with exhibits detailing the ship's construction, preservation, and the lives of those on board. Tickets cost 170 SEK ($16) for adults, and children under 18 enter for free. The museum's dimly lit halls and towering ship create an unforgettable atmosphere, making it a must-visit for anyone curious about history.

A short walk from the Vasa Museum brings you to the ABBA Museum at Djurgårdsvägen 68. Whether you're a lifelong fan or just know the hits, this interactive museum is pure joy. From original costumes and instruments to immersive exhibits where you can virtually join the band on stage, it's a playful yet insightful celebration of Sweden's most famous musical export. Tickets cost 250 SEK ($23), and booking online in advance is recommended, especially during peak travel seasons. The museum's energy is infectious, and even if you're not a die-hard ABBA fan, you'll leave with a smile on your face.

For lunch, Djurgården offers several options, from casual cafes to elegant restaurants. Try Rosendals Trädgård, a garden café serving organic and seasonal dishes, with meals starting at 150 SEK ($14). Dining in their greenhouse amidst flowers and greenery is a delightful experience.

Evening: Archipelago Boat Tour

As the afternoon turns to evening, it's time to explore the Stockholm Archipelago, a collection of over 30,000 islands scattered across the Baltic Sea. One of the best ways to experience this natural wonder is on a boat tour departing from the Strömkajen quay near the Grand Hotel. Companies like Stromma offer evening cruises starting at 340 SEK ($31) for a two-hour journey. These tours often include a guide who shares fascinating insights about the islands' history and ecology.

As you glide through the waters, you'll pass rocky shores, charming red cottages, and lush forests. The light during the evening hours casts a golden glow over the landscape, making it a magical time to be on the water. Some tours offer dinner options on board, allowing you to enjoy a meal with a view. If you prefer to eat after the cruise, return to the city for a meal at Eriks Gondolen, a restaurant near Slussen that offers panoramic views of Stockholm. Their Swedish-inspired dishes start at 250 SEK ($23), and the sunset view over the city is the perfect way to end your day.

Practical Tips

Stockholm's public transport system is efficient and easy to use. A 24-hour SL travel card costs 155 SEK ($14) and covers buses, metro, and ferries, making it a great value for exploring the city. If you prefer walking, the central areas like Gamla Stan and Djurgården are pedestrian-friendly and a joy to navigate on foot.

Summer is the ideal time to visit, with long daylight hours allowing you to pack more into your day. Spring and autumn also have their charms, with fewer crowds and cooler weather adding to the experience.

Day 3: Oslo, Norway

Morning: Viking Ship Museum and Norwegian Maritime History

Start your day by diving into Norway's fascinating Viking heritage at the Viking Ship Museum, located at Huk Aveny 35 on the Bygdøy Peninsula. This world-renowned museum houses some of the best-preserved Viking ships ever discovered, including the Oseberg, Gokstad, and Tune ships, which date back over a thousand years. The sleek, detailed craftsmanship of these vessels is awe-inspiring, offering a glimpse into the maritime expertise and adventurous spirit of the Vikings. In addition to the ships, the museum displays tools, textiles, and artifacts that paint a vivid picture of Viking life. Admission costs 120 NOK ($12), and guided tours are available for an additional fee, providing deeper insights into the exhibits.

To get to the Viking Ship Museum, take the ferry from Oslo City Hall to Bygdøy, a scenic 15-minute ride that offers views of the harbor. Alternatively, buses run regularly from Oslo Central Station. Spend your morning marveling at the exhibits and immersing yourself in Norway's storied past. The museum opens at 10 AM, so arriving early ensures you can enjoy the space before it gets busier.

Afternoon: Aker Brygge and the Oslo Opera House

After exploring the Viking Ship Museum, head back to the city center and make your way to Aker Brygge, a bustling waterfront district brimming with energy. Located along Oslofjord, Aker Brygge is a hub for shopping, dining, and people-watching. Stroll along the boardwalk, where modern architecture meets traditional Norwegian design, and take in the views of boats gliding across the fjord. For lunch, consider dining at Louise Restaurant & Bar, which offers fresh seafood with a Scandinavian twist. A typical meal, like their famous fish soup, costs around 250 NOK ($24), and their outdoor seating provides a perfect view of the harbor.

After lunch, walk or take a short tram ride to the Oslo Opera House, an architectural masterpiece that seems to rise from the waters of the fjord. Located at Kirsten Flagstads Plass 1, this modern icon is known for its sloping marble roof, which invites visitors to climb up for panoramic views of the city and the fjord. Entry to the roof is free, making it a popular spot for locals and tourists alike. If you're interested in exploring the interior, guided tours are available for 130 NOK ($12), offering a behind-the-scenes look at the Opera House's design and backstage areas. The Opera House is also home to world-class performances, so check the schedule in advance if you'd like to catch a show.

Evening: Karl Johans Gate and Oslo's Nightlife

As the afternoon turns to evening, make your way to Karl Johans Gate, Oslo's main pedestrian street. Stretching from Oslo Central Station to the Royal Palace, this lively avenue is lined with shops, cafes, and historical landmarks. Along the way, you'll pass the majestic Stortinget (Parliament) building and the National Theatre. The street is perfect for leisurely strolling, picking up souvenirs, or simply soaking in the city's vibrant atmosphere.

For dinner, treat yourself to a memorable meal at Theatercaféen, a historic restaurant located near the National Theatre at Stortingsgata 24. Known for its elegant ambiance and classic Norwegian dishes, it's a favorite among locals and visitors alike. Their venison steak or Arctic char, paired with a glass of fine wine, provides a delightful end to your day. Dinner here typically costs around 500 NOK ($47) per person.

If you're up for exploring Oslo's nightlife, Aker Brygge and the nearby Tjuvholmen district are lively areas with a range of bars and lounges. Magic Ice Bar, located at Kristian IV's gate 12, offers a unique experience where everything, from the walls to the glasses, is made of ice. Admission, which includes a welcome drink, costs 199 NOK ($18), and the frosty atmosphere is a fun way to cap off your evening.

Practical Tips

Oslo's public transport system is efficient and user-friendly, with trams, buses, and ferries making it easy to get around. A 24-hour Ruter ticket costs 117 NOK ($11) and covers unlimited travel within the central zones. Alternatively, Oslo is a walkable city, with many attractions conveniently located within a short distance of one another.

Summer is an ideal time to visit Oslo, with long daylight hours that let you pack more into your day. However, winter brings its own charm, with a cozy atmosphere and festive decorations adding to the city's appeal.

Day 4: Bergen and the Fjords

Morning: Fløibanen Funicular and Mount Fløyen

Start your day with a trip on the Fløibanen Funicular, one of Bergen's most iconic attractions. The funicular departs from Vetrlidsallmenningen 23, right in the city center, and takes you up to Mount Fløyen in just six minutes. Tickets cost 150 NOK ($14) for a round trip and can be purchased online or at the station. The ride itself is a treat, offering views of the city as you ascend to 320 meters above sea level.

At the summit, you'll be greeted by panoramic views of Bergen, its surrounding mountains, and the fjords beyond. The crisp morning air and sweeping vistas make this the perfect spot for photos or a leisurely coffee at the mountaintop café. If you're feeling adventurous, there are several well-marked hiking trails that begin at Mount Fløyen, ranging from easy walks to more challenging treks. Even a short stroll into the forest reveals serene lakes and lush greenery, giving you a taste of Norway's natural beauty.

After enjoying the views and perhaps a hike, take the funicular back down to the city center. By now, you'll have worked up an appetite, so stop at one of Bergen's cozy cafes for a late breakfast or an early lunch. Café Kippers, located at Georgernes Verft 12, serves up hearty Norwegian dishes with waterfront views. A meal here, such as smoked salmon on rye bread or a bowl of fish soup, costs around 200 NOK ($18).

Afternoon: Exploring Bryggen and the Hanseatic Heritage

Once back in the city, head to Bryggen, Bergen's UNESCO World Heritage Site and one of its most recognizable landmarks. This historic wharf dates back to the 14th century, when it served as a center for trade during the Hanseatic League. The colorful wooden buildings that line the harbor are home to small shops, art galleries, and cafes, making it a delightful place to explore. Stroll through the narrow alleyways between the buildings, where you'll feel as though you've stepped back in time.

To gain deeper insight into Bryggen's history, visit the Hanseatic Museum and Schøtstuene at Finnegården 1A. The museum offers a fascinating look at the lives of Hanseatic merchants and the bustling trade that shaped Bergen's history. Admission costs 120 NOK ($11) and includes access to restored meeting rooms and exhibits showcasing artifacts from the period.

After exploring Bryggen, walk over to the Fish Market (Fisketorget) at Torget 5, just a short distance away. The market is an ideal spot to sample fresh seafood, such as prawns, crab, or Bergen's famous fish soup. You can enjoy a light snack or pick up something for later. The Fish Market is also a vibrant place to soak in the local culture, with friendly vendors eager to share their stories and recommendations.

Evening: Sognefjord Cruise

No trip to Bergen is complete without venturing into the fjords, and an evening cruise on the Sognefjord is the perfect way to cap off your day. The Sognefjord, known as the "King of the Fjords," is the longest and deepest fjord in Norway, stretching over 200 kilometers inland. Cruises typically depart from Bergen Harbor in the late afternoon or early evening, making them a convenient addition to your itinerary.

Fjord Tours offers a popular round-trip cruise to Nærøyfjord, a branch of the Sognefjord and a UNESCO World Heritage Site. Tickets cost around 1,000 NOK ($92) for a three-hour journey. The boat is equipped with indoor seating and outdoor decks, so you can enjoy the scenery regardless of the weather. As the boat glides through the calm waters, you'll be surrounded by towering cliffs, cascading waterfalls, and picturesque villages that seem untouched by time.

The experience is as serene as it is awe-inspiring, with the fjord's stillness amplifying the beauty of the landscape. Don't forget to bring a jacket, as the temperature can drop in the evening, even in summer. Many cruises offer light refreshments on board, but you're also welcome to bring snacks or drinks purchased earlier at the Fish Market.

As the cruise returns to Bergen, the city's lights twinkling against the darkening sky create a magical view, making for a perfect end to the day. Once back on land, consider stopping by one of Bergen's atmospheric bars for a nightcap. Pingvinen, located at Vaskerelven 14, is a cozy spot offering Norwegian craft beers and traditional snacks. A pint costs around 120 NOK ($11), and the warm ambiance makes it a favorite among locals and visitors alike.

Practical Tips

Bergen's compact city center makes it easy to get around on foot, but public transport options like buses and the Bybanen light rail are also available. A 24-hour public transport pass costs 100 NOK ($9) and includes unlimited travel within the city.

Summer is the best time to visit, with long daylight hours that allow you to explore the fjords and enjoy Bergen's outdoor attractions. However, Bergen is known for its unpredictable weather, so bring a waterproof jacket and sturdy shoes, regardless of the season.

Day 5: Helsinki, Finland

Morning: Exploring Suomenlinna Fortress

Start your day with a visit to Suomenlinna, a UNESCO World Heritage Site and one of Helsinki's most iconic attractions. This sea fortress, built in the 18th century, spans several islands and is just a 15-minute ferry ride from the city center. Ferries depart regularly from the Market Square (Kauppatori), with a round-trip ticket costing 5 EUR ($5.50). The short journey offers scenic views of Helsinki's harbor, setting the tone for the day ahead.

Upon arrival, you'll find yourself surrounded by picturesque landscapes, historic buildings, and winding paths perfect for exploration. Start at the Visitor Center, where you can pick up a map and learn about the fortress's history through interactive exhibits. Admission to the fortress itself is free, though guided tours are available for 12 EUR ($13), offering deeper insights into Suomenlinna's strategic importance during various conflicts.

Wander through the fortress's bastions and tunnels, and visit the Ehrensvärd Museum, which provides a fascinating look at life during the fortress's early days. Don't miss the King's Gate, an iconic symbol of Suomenlinna, offering panoramic views of the sea. For a mid-morning snack, stop by Café Vanille, a charming spot located in a 19th-century wooden building. Enjoy a fresh cinnamon bun and a cup of Finnish coffee for around 8 EUR ($8.50) before heading back to the city.

Afternoon: Helsinki's Design District

After returning to the mainland, spend the afternoon exploring Helsinki's Design District, a vibrant hub of creativity and innovation located in the neighborhoods of Punavuori, Kaartinkaupunki, and Kamppi. This area is home to over 200 design-focused businesses, including boutiques, galleries, and studios, making it a must-visit for anyone with an appreciation for craftsmanship and aesthetics.

Begin your exploration at the Design Museum, located at Korkeavuorenkatu 23. Tickets cost 12 EUR ($13), and the museum showcases Finnish design through the ages, from iconic brands like Marimekko and Iittala to contemporary innovations. Afterward, wander the district's streets, where you'll find an array of shops selling everything from minimalist furniture to handcrafted jewelry. Stores like Artek, known for its sleek Scandinavian designs, and Lokal, a gallery and shop featuring work by Finnish artists, are particularly worth visiting.

For lunch, head to the Design District's Ravintola Nolla, located at Fredrikinkatu 22. This zero-waste restaurant combines sustainability with exceptional flavors, offering a seasonal menu that highlights local ingredients. A three-course lunch costs around 45 EUR ($47), and the creative presentation of each dish reflects the district's artistic spirit.

Evening: Traditional Finnish Sauna and Seaside Dining

No visit to Helsinki would be complete without experiencing a traditional Finnish sauna, a cornerstone of the country's culture and a deeply relaxing way to end the day. Löyly, located at Hernesaarenranta 4, is a contemporary public sauna that blends modern design with the timeless tradition of sweating it out by the water. The striking wooden building offers both traditional smoke and wood-heated saunas, as well as direct access to the Baltic Sea for a refreshing plunge. A two-hour sauna session costs 21 EUR ($22), and reservations are recommended, especially during peak hours.

As you sit in the warm glow of the sauna, with views of the sea stretching out before you, you'll feel the stress of the day melt away. The Finns believe that the sauna is a place to cleanse not just the body but also the mind, and Löyly provides the perfect environment to embrace this philosophy.

After your sauna session, stay at Löyly for dinner at their waterfront restaurant, which serves a menu inspired by Finnish and Nordic flavors. Dishes like smoked fish, seasonal vegetables, and rye bread are elevated with creative touches, and mains start at 25 EUR ($26). Dining on the terrace as the sun sets over the sea is a magical experience, capturing the essence of Helsinki's connection to nature.

Practical Tips

Helsinki's compact size makes it easy to get around on foot or by public transport. A single tram or bus ticket costs 2.80 EUR ($3), while a day pass for unlimited travel within the city is 9 EUR ($9.50). Ferries to Suomenlinna are included in the day pass, making it a convenient and cost-effective option.

Summer, with its long daylight hours, is the ideal time to visit, allowing you to fully enjoy outdoor activities and the city's vibrant atmosphere. However, Helsinki's charm extends into the colder months, when cozy cafes and the warmth of the sauna offer a welcome retreat from the chill.

Day 6: Reykjavik, Iceland

Morning: Hallgrímskirkja and Panoramic Views

Start your day in Reykjavik with a visit to Hallgrímskirkja, Iceland's most recognizable landmark. Located at Hallgrímstorg 1, this stunning Lutheran church towers over the city at 74.5 meters tall, its design inspired by the country's basalt lava flows. Arrive early to beat the crowds and enjoy the serene beauty of this architectural masterpiece. Admission to the church is free, but access to the tower costs 1,200 ISK ($9). Taking the elevator up to the top rewards you with breathtaking panoramic views of Reykjavik's colorful rooftops, the surrounding mountains, and the vast Atlantic Ocean. It's the perfect spot to capture photos and orient yourself to the city.

After taking in the views, wander around the area to soak in the local vibe. You'll find charming streets filled with shops, cafes, and galleries. Stop by Brauð & Co., a local bakery near the church, for a delicious cinnamon bun or croissant paired with a strong Icelandic coffee. A pastry and coffee cost around 1,200 ISK ($9), providing a quick and satisfying breakfast before your next adventure.

Late Morning: Harpa Concert Hall and Waterfront Stroll

From Hallgrímskirkja, take a leisurely 15-minute walk down Laugavegur, Reykjavik's main shopping street, to Harpa Concert Hall. This striking glass building, located at Austurbakki 2, is an architectural gem that reflects Iceland's creative spirit. Designed by artist Olafur Eliasson, Harpa's façade glimmers like a kaleidoscope as it captures and refracts light. Step inside to explore its modern interiors, which host concerts, cultural events, and art installations.

If you have time, join a guided tour of Harpa to learn about its design and significance. Tours cost 2,000 ISK ($15) and last about 30 minutes. Even if you don't catch a concert, simply wandering the halls and admiring the play of light through the glass panels is a treat. Afterward, take a stroll along the nearby waterfront, where you'll encounter the Sun Voyager, a striking steel sculpture that represents a Viking ship and symbolizes Iceland's adventurous spirit. It's a great spot for photos and a moment of reflection with the sea breeze in your hair.

Afternoon: Golden Circle Tour

After exploring Reykjavik's cultural landmarks, it's time to venture into Iceland's natural wonders on a Golden Circle tour. This iconic route covers three of Iceland's most famous attractions: Þingvellir National Park, Geysir Geothermal Area, and Gullfoss Waterfall. Many tour operators, such as Reykjavik Excursions or Arctic Adventures, offer day trips departing from the city. Prices range from 10,000 to 15,000 ISK ($75–$110), including transportation and a guide.

The first stop, Þingvellir National Park, is about a 40-minute drive from Reykjavik. This UNESCO World Heritage Site is not only geologically significant—sitting on the rift between the Eurasian and North American tectonic plates—but also historically important as the site of Iceland's first parliament, established in 930 AD. Stroll through the park's dramatic landscapes, marveling at fissures, waterfalls, and crystal-clear water-filled ravines.

Next, visit the Geysir Geothermal Area, home to the famous Strokkur geyser. Strokkur erupts every few minutes, shooting water up to 20 meters into the air, making it a thrilling natural spectacle. Nearby, you'll find bubbling mud pots and steaming vents that showcase Iceland's geothermal activity. Grab a snack or coffee at the visitor center before heading to the final stop.

The tour concludes at Gullfoss, one of Iceland's most iconic waterfalls. This two-tiered cascade roars as it plunges into a canyon, creating misty rainbows on sunny days. Take the well-maintained paths to viewpoints that offer incredible perspectives of the falls. The raw power and beauty of Gullfoss are unforgettable, and it's easy to see why it's one of Iceland's most beloved natural attractions.

Evening: Return to Reykjavik and Dining

After a day filled with natural wonders, return to Reykjavik in the early evening. For dinner, treat yourself to a meal at Sjávargrillið, located at Skólavörðustígur 14, just a short walk from Hallgrímskirkja. This cozy restaurant specializes in Icelandic seafood, with dishes like Arctic char and langoustine prepared with a creative flair. A main course costs around 4,000 ISK ($30), and the warm ambiance makes it the perfect spot to unwind after a busy day.

If you're in the mood for something more casual, try Icelandic Fish and Chips, located at Tryggvagata 11. This relaxed eatery serves sustainably sourced fish paired with crispy potato wedges and delicious skyr-based dips. A meal here costs around 2,500 ISK ($18), and it's a local favorite for good reason.

Practical Tips

The Golden Circle tour is best enjoyed in clear weather, so check the forecast and dress appropriately. Layers are essential, as Iceland's weather can change rapidly, even in summer. Comfortable walking shoes are a must, especially for exploring Þingvellir and Gullfoss.

Reykjavik is a compact city, and walking is the best way to get around its central attractions. If needed, buses are available, with single tickets costing 490 ISK ($4). For added convenience, some Golden Circle tours include hotel pick-up and drop-off.

Day 7: Iceland's Natural Wonders

Morning: The Blue Lagoon

Start your day with a visit to Iceland's iconic Blue Lagoon, located in the heart of a lava field in Grindavik, about 45 minutes from Reykjavik. This geothermal spa is world-famous for its milky-blue waters rich in minerals like silica and sulfur, known for their soothing and rejuvenating properties. Book your entry in advance, as the lagoon is extremely popular. Standard tickets start at 8,500 ISK ($60), which includes entrance, a silica mud mask, and a drink of your choice. Upgrade packages with robes and additional treatments are available for a more luxurious experience.

Arriving early ensures a peaceful start to your day as you soak in the warm, steamy waters surrounded by rugged volcanic terrain. Take your time to apply the silica mud mask, which leaves your skin glowing, and relax in the lagoon's tranquil atmosphere. The Blue Lagoon also features in-water massage treatments, saunas, and a swim-up bar for those who wish to elevate their experience further.

For breakfast or a light snack before or after your soak, stop by the Blue Café, which serves fresh pastries and coffee for around 2,000 ISK ($15). If you're looking for a more indulgent dining experience, the on-site Lava Restaurant offers modern Icelandic cuisine in a setting carved into the lava itself. A two-course lunch costs about 7,000 ISK ($50), and the stunning views of the lagoon make it well worth the price.

Afternoon: Exploring Lava Fields

After a relaxing morning at the Blue Lagoon, it's time to delve into Iceland's geological wonders by exploring the surrounding lava fields. These ancient landscapes, formed by volcanic eruptions thousands of years ago, are otherworldly in their beauty, with jagged rocks covered in moss and an eerie sense of tranquility. Rent a car or join a guided tour to fully immerse yourself in this unique environment.

One of the best places to experience Iceland's volcanic heritage is the nearby Reykjanes Peninsula. Stop at the Bridge Between Continents, a symbolic structure spanning the Eurasian and North American tectonic plates, offering a tangible connection to Iceland's position on the Mid-Atlantic Ridge. Admission is free, and walking across this "bridge" feels like stepping between two worlds.

Another highlight is the Krýsuvík geothermal area, where steaming vents, bubbling mud pots, and colorful mineral deposits create a landscape that seems almost alien. Admission is free, and there are wooden walkways and viewing platforms for safe exploration. The scent of sulfur adds to the authenticity of the experience, reminding you of Iceland's raw geothermal energy.

For a closer look at Iceland's volcanic past, visit the Lava Centre in Hvolsvöllur, about an hour's drive from the Reykjanes Peninsula. This interactive museum offers fascinating exhibits on Iceland's volcanic and seismic activity, including simulations of eruptions. Tickets cost 3,900 ISK ($28), and the experience provides valuable context for understanding the forces that have shaped the island's landscapes.

Evening: Northern Lights Tour

As night falls, prepare for one of Iceland's most magical experiences: a Northern Lights tour. From September to April, the aurora borealis transforms Iceland's skies into a canvas of swirling greens, pinks, and purples. While sightings depend on weather and solar activity, a clear night with minimal light pollution increases your chances.

Many operators, such as Arctic Adventures or Reykjavik Excursions, offer guided Northern Lights tours departing from Reykjavik in the evening. Prices range from 9,000 to 12,000 ISK ($65–$90) and include transportation to optimal viewing locations based on real-time aurora forecasts. Guides provide insights into the science and folklore surrounding the Northern Lights, enhancing the experience.

Your guide will take you to remote areas away from city lights, often along the Reykjanes Peninsula or into the countryside. Dress warmly, as temperatures can drop significantly at night, especially when standing still to watch the lights. Bring a thermos of hot chocolate or tea to stay cozy and a good camera with a tripod to capture the beauty of the aurora.

The moment the lights appear is nothing short of magical. Waves of green ripple across the sky, occasionally joined by hints of red or purple, creating an ethereal display that feels almost unreal. Even if the lights are faint, the experience of standing under Iceland's vast, star-filled sky is humbling and unforgettable.

Practical Tips

Getting to the Blue Lagoon is easy, with regular shuttles running from Reykjavik and Keflavik International Airport. A round-trip transfer costs about 5,000 ISK ($35). If you're driving, parking is free, and the journey takes less than an hour from the city.

For the Northern Lights tour, operators typically pick up and drop off guests at central Reykjavik hotels, ensuring a hassle-free experience. Dress in layers, including thermal undergarments, insulated jackets, hats, gloves, and sturdy boots, to stay comfortable throughout the evening.

PRACTICAL INFORMATION AND TIPS

Transportation in Scandinavia

Transportation in Scandinavia is efficient, reliable, and well-designed to help travelers explore the region with ease. Whether you're gliding through scenic landscapes on a train, cruising across fjords on a ferry, or navigating bustling cities with public transport passes, Scandinavia offers a seamless travel experience.

Train Networks

Scandinavia's train networks are among the best in Europe, offering comfortable and scenic journeys between major cities and picturesque countryside. In Sweden, SJ (Swedish Railways) operates high-speed trains like the X2000, which connect cities like Stockholm, Gothenburg, and Malmö. A one-way ticket from Stockholm to Gothenburg starts at 295 SEK ($27) if booked in advance, and the journey takes about three hours.

Norway's train system, operated by Vy, is known for its spectacular routes. The Oslo to Bergen line, often called one of the most beautiful train journeys in the world, takes you through mountains, valleys, and fjords in just under seven hours. Tickets for this journey start at 249 NOK ($23). The Flåm Railway, a shorter but equally stunning route, connects Myrdal to Flåm and offers breathtaking views of waterfalls and steep cliffs.

In Denmark, DSB trains connect Copenhagen to other parts of the country and neighboring Germany. The Øresundståg regional trains provide a convenient link between Copenhagen and Malmö, with tickets costing around 130 DKK ($19) for the 40-minute journey.

For longer trips across Scandinavia, consider the Eurail Scandinavia Pass, which allows unlimited train travel in Denmark, Sweden, Norway, and Finland for a set number of days. Prices start at €200 ($210) for three days of travel within a month, offering flexibility and savings for those planning multiple journeys.

Ferries

Ferries play a vital role in connecting Scandinavia's cities, islands, and neighboring countries. In Norway, Hurtigruten ferries operate along the stunning coastal route from Bergen to Kirkenes, often referred to as the "world's most beautiful sea voyage." Prices start at 3,000 NOK ($280) for a one-way trip, with shorter segments also available.

In Denmark, ferries connect the main islands of Zealand, Funen, and Jutland, as well as routes to Germany and Sweden. DFDS Seaways operates a popular overnight ferry from Copenhagen to Oslo, combining transportation with a mini-cruise experience. Cabins start at 1,200 DKK ($175) for two people.

Sweden and Finland are linked by ferries crossing the Baltic Sea, with Viking Line and Tallink Silja offering routes between Stockholm and Helsinki. These ferries are known for their amenities, including restaurants, entertainment, and duty-free shopping. Prices for a basic cabin start at €40 ($42) per person, depending on the season.

Iceland also relies on ferries for domestic travel and connections to the Faroe Islands and Denmark. The Smyril Line operates a route from Seyðisfjörður in Iceland to Hirtshals, Denmark, with prices starting at €160 ($170) for a one-way trip.

Budget Airlines

For faster travel between Scandinavian countries or to remote locations, budget airlines like Norwegian Air Shuttle, SAS Go Light, and Ryanair offer affordable options. Norwegian Air Shuttle is particularly popular, with frequent flights between cities such as Oslo, Stockholm, and Copenhagen. Tickets can be as low as €30 ($32) if booked early, making it a competitive alternative to trains for long distances.

SAS (Scandinavian Airlines) provides a mix of budget-friendly and premium options, with domestic and international routes across Scandinavia and beyond. Keep an eye on deals during low seasons, which can make flying even more economical.

Public Transport Passes in Scandinavian Cities

Scandinavian cities are known for their excellent public transportation systems, making it easy to explore without a car. In Copenhagen, the Copenhagen Card offers unlimited access to buses, trains, and metro lines, as well as free entry to over 80 attractions. Prices start at 419 DKK ($60) for a 24-hour pass.

In Stockholm, the SL Access card provides unlimited travel on buses, metro, trams, and ferries. A 24-hour card costs 165 SEK ($16), while a 7-day pass is available for 450 SEK ($43). The Stockholm Pass combines public transport with free entry to attractions, making it a great option for tourists.

Oslo's Ruter public transport system includes buses, trams, ferries, and the metro, all accessible with a single ticket. A 24-hour pass costs 117 NOK ($11), while weekly passes are priced at 323 NOK ($30). Similarly, Helsinki's HSL system offers travel passes starting at €8 ($9) for a day, covering buses, trams, metro, and ferries.

Money and Budgeting

Nordic Currencies and Exchange Rates

Denmark: The official currency is the Danish krone (DKK). One US dollar is roughly equivalent to 6.8 DKK.

Sweden: Sweden uses the Swedish krona (SEK), with one US dollar equal to about 10.5 SEK.

Norway: The currency is the Norwegian krone (NOK), with one US dollar worth approximately 11 NOK.

Iceland: The Icelandic króna (ISK) is used here, and one US dollar equals about 135 ISK.

Exchange rates can fluctuate, so it's a good idea to check the current rates before your trip using online tools or apps like XE Currency. While Finland uses the euro (EUR), travelers to the other Nordic countries will need to prepare for separate currencies.

Exchanging Money

Although currency exchange counters are available at airports and major cities, they often charge high fees. To get better rates, consider withdrawing cash directly from ATMs upon arrival. If you need to exchange cash, local banks and post offices typically offer more favorable rates than airport kiosks or standalone exchange booths.

It's also worth noting that Scandinavia is moving toward a cashless society. Many establishments, especially in Sweden, no longer accept cash at all, so you may not need to exchange much currency if you plan to rely on cards.

Using Credit Cards

Credit cards are widely accepted throughout Scandinavia, making them a convenient way to pay for most purchases. Visa and Mastercard are the most commonly used, while American Express and Diners Club are less frequently accepted. From restaurants and public transport to small shops and attractions, cards are the preferred payment method.

For the best experience, make sure your credit card is equipped with chip-and-PIN technology, as this is standard in Scandinavia. Contactless payment options, like Apple Pay and Google Pay, are also widely available and can be particularly convenient for small transactions.

Before you travel, notify your bank or credit card provider of your plans to avoid any issues with flagged transactions. Additionally, check whether your card charges foreign transaction fees, as these can add up quickly. If your card has high fees, consider applying for a travel-friendly credit card that offers no foreign transaction charges and rewards for international spending.

ATMs in Scandinavia

ATMs are plentiful in Scandinavian cities and towns, making it easy to withdraw local currency as needed. Major banks like Danske Bank in Denmark, Swedbank in Sweden, and DNB in Norway operate reliable ATMs that accept international debit and credit cards. Look for ATMs with the logos of Visa, Mastercard, or Cirrus to ensure compatibility with your card.

When using ATMs, opt to withdraw in the local currency rather than your home currency. This avoids unfavorable conversion rates and extra fees imposed by the ATM. Keep an eye out for potential service fees, though many Scandinavian ATMs do not charge for withdrawals. Your home bank may still apply an international ATM fee, so check with them beforehand.

For security, use ATMs located in well-lit, public areas or inside bank branches. Always shield your PIN and monitor your bank statements for any unauthorized transactions.

Budgeting Tips for Scandinavia

City Passes: In cities like Copenhagen, Stockholm, and Oslo, passes offer unlimited public transport and free entry to attractions, saving both money and time.

Supermarkets: Eating out can be costly, so consider shopping at local grocery stores like Coop (Denmark), ICA (Sweden), or Rema 1000 (Norway) for affordable meals and snacks.

Free Attractions: Many museums, parks, and natural wonders are free to visit, allowing you to enjoy the region's beauty without added costs.

Transportation: Public transport is efficient and cost-effective. Look into travel passes for trains and buses to save on individual fares.

Language and Communication

English Proficiency in Scandinavia

Scandinavians are renowned for their excellent command of English, often starting language education at a young age. In Denmark, Sweden, and Norway, English proficiency is particularly high, with most people fluent enough to hold conversations and assist with directions, making these countries some of the easiest to navigate for English-speaking travelers.

Finland and Iceland also boast high levels of English proficiency, though Finnish and Icelandic are more distinct from the other Scandinavian languages. In remote areas, English might not be as widely spoken, but in cities and towns, you'll find that most locals are happy to communicate in English.

Despite the ease of using English, learning a few basic phrases in the local language is always appreciated and can enhance your interactions with locals. It shows respect for the culture and adds a personal touch to your travels.

Basic Phrases in Scandinavian Languages

Greetings and Politeness

Hello:
- Danish: Hej (pronounced "hi")
- Swedish: Hej (pronounced "hey")
- Norwegian: Hei (pronounced "hi")
- Finnish: Hei (pronounced "hey")
- Icelandic: Halló (pronounced "hah-lo")

Good morning:
- Danish: Godmorgen
- Swedish: God morgon
- Norwegian: God morgen

- Finnish: Hyvää huomenta
- Icelandic: Góðan daginn

Please:
- Danish: Vær venlig
- Swedish: Snälla
- Norwegian: Vær så snill
- Finnish: Ole hyvä
- Icelandic: Vinsamlegast

Thank you:
- Danish: Tak
- Swedish: Tack
- Norwegian: Takk
- Finnish: Kiitos
- Icelandic: Takk

Yes/No:
- Danish: Ja/Nej
- Swedish: Ja/Nej
- Norwegian: Ja/Nei
- Finnish: Kyllä/Ei
- Icelandic: Já/Nei

Practical Phrases
- Do you speak English?:
- Danish: Taler du engelsk?
- Swedish: Talar du engelska?
- Norwegian: Snakker du engelsk?
- Finnish: Puhutko englantia?
- Icelandic: Talarðu ensku?

Excuse me:
- Danish: Undskyld mig
- Swedish: Ursäkta
- Norwegian: Unnskyld
- Finnish: Anteeksi
- Icelandic: Afsakið

How much does it cost?:
- Danish: Hvor meget koster det?
- Swedish: Hur mycket kostar det?
- Norwegian: Hvor mye koster det?
- Finnish: Paljonko tämä maksaa?
- Icelandic: Hvað kostar þetta?

Where is the bathroom?:
- Danish: Hvor er toilettet?
- Swedish: Var är toaletten?
- Norwegian: Hvor er toalettet?
- Finnish: Missä on vessa?
- Icelandic: Hvar er klósettið?

Help!:
- Danish: Hjælp!
- Swedish: Hjälp!
- Norwegian: Hjelp!
- Finnish: Apu!
- Icelandic: Hjálp!

Language Similarities and Tips

Danish, Swedish, and Norwegian are closely related North Germanic languages, meaning they share many similarities. If you learn basic phrases in one language, you'll often find they are nearly identical in the other two. For example, "thank you" (tack/takk) and "good morning" (god morgon/god morgen) are almost interchangeable. This linguistic overlap can be particularly helpful if you're traveling across multiple Scandinavian countries.

Finnish and Icelandic, however, are distinct. Finnish is part of the Uralic language family and is unrelated to the other Scandinavian languages, while Icelandic, though a North Germanic language, has remained relatively unchanged since the Viking Age, making it unique even among its linguistic cousins.

When trying out local phrases, don't worry too much about perfect pronunciation. Scandinavians are generally understanding and appreciate the effort. In Iceland, for instance, even a simple "Takk" can bring a warm smile.

Practical Tools for Communication

To make communication even smoother, consider downloading language apps like Google Translate, which includes offline options for Scandinavian languages. Phrasebooks and travel guides with language sections are also great companions for your trip.

In restaurants, shops, and public transport, signage is often available in English alongside the local language, especially in tourist areas. However, learning to recognize key words like "exit" (udgang/utgang) or "entrance" (indgang/inngang) can still be useful.

Safety and Travel Tips

Emergency Contacts

Each Scandinavian country has an efficient emergency response system, and dialing 112 will connect you to police, fire, and medical services across Denmark, Sweden, Norway, Finland, and Iceland. It's a unified number that works throughout the European Union and ensures quick assistance in emergencies.

- **Denmark**: 112 for emergencies; non-emergency police: 114.
- **Sweden**: 112 for emergencies; non-emergency police: 114 14.
- **Norway**: 112 for police, 113 for medical emergencies, and 110 for fire services.
- **Finland**: 112 for all emergencies; non-emergency police: 0295 419 800.

- **Iceland**: 112 for emergencies; Reykjavik police non-emergency line: +354 444 1000.

Healthcare Services

Scandinavia boasts excellent healthcare systems, and travelers can access high-quality medical care if needed. Citizens of the European Union (EU) or European Economic Area (EEA) should carry their European Health Insurance Card (EHIC), which provides access to necessary healthcare during their stay.

For non-EU/EEA travelers, comprehensive travel insurance is strongly recommended. Healthcare costs for uninsured visitors can be expensive, especially for emergencies. In case of minor ailments, pharmacies are well-stocked, and pharmacists can often provide advice and over-the-counter remedies. Pharmacies in Scandinavia are marked with a green cross or the word "Apotek."

In major cities like Copenhagen, Stockholm, Oslo, Helsinki, and Reykjavik, hospitals and clinics are readily available. For non-emergencies, private clinics are a faster option, though they may require payment upfront.

Areas to Avoid

Copenhagen, Denmark: While generally safe, the Nørrebro and Vesterbro neighborhoods can feel a bit edgy after dark due to occasional gang-related activity. Stick to well-lit streets and popular areas.

Stockholm, Sweden: Avoid spending time in isolated parts of the suburbs, such as Rinkeby or Tensta, especially late at night. The city center and tourist districts are safe and well-monitored.

Oslo, Norway: The central station area can attract petty crime, particularly after dark. Exercise caution and avoid flashing valuables.

Helsinki, Finland: The Kallio district has a bohemian vibe but can be rowdy during late-night hours, especially around bars.

Reykjavik, Iceland: Iceland's capital is exceptionally safe, but always take basic precautions, particularly around busy nightlife spots where alcohol-fueled incidents occasionally occur.

Common Scams

Pickpocketing: In busy areas like train stations, shopping streets, and tourist attractions, pickpockets may target distracted travelers. Keep your valuables close and avoid leaving bags unattended.

Fake Charity Collectors: In tourist-heavy spots, you might encounter individuals asking for donations for dubious charities. Politely decline and move on.

Taxi Overcharges: While taxis in Scandinavia are generally reputable, some drivers may try to inflate fares for tourists. Always use licensed taxis and confirm the estimated cost before starting your trip. Ridesharing apps like Bolt and Uber are available in major cities and provide transparent pricing.

ATM Skimming: Rare but possible, skimming devices may be placed on ATMs to steal card details. Use ATMs located inside banks for added security.

General Safety Tips

Be Weather-Wise: Scandinavia's weather can change quickly, particularly in Norway, Iceland, and Finland. Always check forecasts and dress in layers, especially if you're heading into rural or mountainous areas.

Respect Nature: Whether hiking in Norway's fjords or exploring Iceland's geothermal landscapes, follow local guidelines, stick to marked paths, and never underestimate the power of nature.

Follow Local Laws: Alcohol regulations vary across the region. For example, in Sweden and Norway, only government-operated stores (Systembolaget and Vinmonopolet) sell alcohol above 3.5% ABV. Public drinking is also restricted in many areas.

Stay Connected: Ensure your phone works internationally, and consider purchasing a local SIM card for reliable connectivity. This is particularly useful for accessing maps, contacting emergency services, or staying updated on weather conditions.

Cultural Etiquette

Understanding local customs and social norms can help you navigate interactions and experiences with ease, leaving a positive impression on the friendly and welcoming locals. From tipping practices to dining manners and unique traditions, here's what you need to know about cultural etiquette in Scandinavia.

Tipping Customs

Tipping in Scandinavia is different from many other parts of the world. In Denmark, Sweden, Norway, Finland, and Iceland, service charges are typically included in restaurant bills, and tipping is not obligatory. However, rounding up the bill or leaving a small tip of 5–10% as a gesture of appreciation for excellent service is common, particularly in fine dining establishments or cafes.

In bars, tipping is also not expected, but leaving the change from your round or rounding up the bill is appreciated. For taxi rides, it's customary to round up to the nearest whole amount or add a few extra coins, but this is entirely at your discretion. Hotel staff, such as bellhops or housekeeping, generally do not expect tips, though small gratuities are welcome for exceptional service.

While tipping is modest in Scandinavia, what matters more is politeness and a genuine "thank you" (or "takk" in Norwegian, "tack" in Swedish, and "kiitos" in Finnish) for services rendered.

Dining Manners

Seating Etiquette: Wait to be seated or follow the host's instructions if you're dining in someone's home. At restaurants, reservations are often recommended, especially in major cities.

Knife and Fork Usage: Scandinavians often use the European style of dining, where the fork remains in the left hand and the knife in the right throughout the meal. Cutting food into small bites before eating is considered polite.

Wait for Toasts: In Norway and Sweden, it's common to wait for the host to make the first toast, often with the word "Skål!" (pronounced "skoal"). Maintain eye contact with your companions during the toast as a sign of respect.

Bread and Butter: In Denmark, it's traditional to eat open-faced sandwiches (*smørrebrød*) with utensils rather than picking them up with your hands.

Paying the Bill: Splitting the bill is common practice among friends, so don't be surprised if your dining companions suggest going "Dutch."

Local Traditions

Midsummer Celebrations: In Sweden and Finland, Midsummer is a highlight of the year, celebrated with dancing around the maypole, singing, and feasting on pickled herring, potatoes, and strawberries. If you're invited to join, participating in these traditions is warmly welcomed.

Hygge and Fika: In Denmark, "hygge" (coziness and comfort) is a way of life, while in Sweden, "fika" refers to a coffee break accompanied by pastries and good conversation. Both emphasize slowing down and appreciating the moment.

Equality and Modesty: Scandinavians value equality and humility. Boasting or overly assertive behavior is frowned upon, and it's important to show respect for others' opinions and personal space.

Social Norms

Politeness and Reserved Behavior: Scandinavians are generally reserved but friendly. Greetings are often understated, such as a simple handshake or nod. Personal space is respected, and standing too close to someone you've just met may feel intrusive.

Punctuality: Being on time is highly valued. Whether it's for a dinner invitation or a business meeting, arriving late is considered disrespectful.

Sustainability: Environmental awareness is deeply ingrained in Scandinavian culture. Recycling, conserving energy, and using public transportation are common practices. Visitors are encouraged to follow suit, such as bringing reusable bags and avoiding unnecessary waste.

Quietness in Public Spaces: Scandinavians appreciate quiet environments, especially on public transport. Loud conversations or phone calls can draw unwanted attention.